BUSINESS REMASTERED

GW00645581

BUSINESS REMASTERED

ALASTAIR DRYBURGH

bookshaker

First Published in Great Britain 2012
by www.BookShaker.com

CONTENTS

WHERE TO START, AND WHY YOU SHOULDN'T READ ALL THIS BOOK

Remember the Avis slogan? "We're Number Two We try harder"

It's a great slogan, but I'm not so sure about its value as a business philosophy. Avis have been trying harder for as long as I can remember – a long time now – and they're still only Number Two.

To me, it seems only fair that if you do try harder, you should be Number One. That is what this book is about. Outperforming competitors in today's difficult, volatile and confusing environment needs more than trying hard – it needs careful thought, a superior process, better information.

If there's one message here, it's that preparation and thought will multiply the impact of what you do while greatly reducing the amount of effort involved. There's no direct relationship between effort and result. Easy moves can produce dramatic results. Hard, unpleasant work may turn out to be quite futile, or even make things worse. Do the right things in the right order, and you may even find that you don't have to address the hardest challenges at all.

That's why the first four chapters of this book are about tools, techniques and planning. Read all of these before you start work. After that, we move on to the specific areas on which one could (emphasise could) act. You don't need to act in all of these areas, or even necessarily read the relevant chapters.

Chapter One

Getting into the Right Mindset

It's Not Just What You Do, But How You Do It

Before starting work, it's worth spending time getting into the right mindset. With most business activity, we tend to assume, at least unconsciously, that we know more or less what we need to do, and that good results flow from working hard and doing things well. That's probably true for most of what we do, but when it comes to performance improvement the truth is something else. There is no particular relationship between the amount of effort expended and the result produced. What makes the difference is how effectively we choose what we do.

Case Study – Efficiency vs Effectiveness

I once worked for a marketing consultancy which suffered from a very common service business problem – lots of work, enthusiastic clients, everyone very busy but struggling to make an adequate profit. We tried to increase the efficiency of our project management with project management training and investment in systems. Effort: large. Results: minimal.

There were probably two reasons for this. The first was that our business was based on being very responsive to clients, and clients were not very organised. A lot of the apparent chaos in our project management was the result of us responding to our clients' chaotic style. They didn't give much thought to planning and organising their work to make things easy for us – we were regularly getting them out of trouble. The second reason was that we were a "creative" business and ideas like discipline and efficiency didn't have much appeal.

Fortunately, at the same time as we were struggling to improve project management we did something else which had a dramatic effect. We simply analysed the profitability of the work we had done over the previous two years, and found some very interesting patterns. The most significant of these was that we were not in a single business, as we had thought, but were in fact in two very different ones. One of these could be characterised as "high value expert service" and the other as "outsourcing basic tasks."

The high value service was to help a pharmaceutical company marketing manager process a mass of scientific data and develop from it marketing messages which could be robustly supported by papers published in scientific journals. This was very valuable, and nobody in the client company could do it themselves. We were very well paid for this sort of work.

The outsourcing work was different. Here the scientific content was lower and the clients felt it was only time constraints that stopped them doing the work themselves. In this case we were valued and paid less.

One of these two businesses was clearly dramatically more profitable for us that the other, and when we understood this, we were able to make choices.

We concentrated on selling more of the highly profitable "expert" work and de-emphasised the "outsourcing". Where we did take on outsourcing work we took a hard line on pricing. The result of these two decisions was to raise profitability overall by 25% in nine months, without any great effort.

Some of the principles of effectiveness:

The Principle of Leverage

Leverage is the relationship between the effort expended and the result produced. The principle of leverage says that different actions offer very different amounts of leverage. Further, there are always ways of increasing leverage. Don't stop at the first idea you have. Look for the higher-leveraged alternative before taking action.

Here are some clues to help you find the points of greatest leverage.

Taking decisions usually gives higher leverage than changing behaviour

This explains the power of Jack Welch's famous prescription to GE, "Be Number One or Number Two in your market or get out".

He could have said "Be the most efficient producer in your market or get out", but he didn't. (He did take some actions in that direction, but they came later.) He knew that there was no point in striving to become more efficient in a market that was inherently unattractive.

Changes involving smaller numbers of people usually give higher leverage than changes involving larger numbers of people

Obvious, but often forgotten. This is one reason why changes to pricing can be very highly leveraged. In most businesses, relatively few people take decisions on pricing – most just use the price list or apply the model.

Changes to systems and processes can give high leverage.

This doesn't apply to computer systems, but to any procedure or process. The leverage comes from making a change once and seeing it applied time after time as the new process is applied.

Changes that go with the grain give higher leverage.

Don't fight organisational culture if you don't have to. In the case study it was always going to be hard to apply project management methodology. In an engineering business it would have been easier, but we were dealing with creatives who took a very different approach to work. The fact that they didn't much care about how their work was priced was not a problem but an opportunity, since it meant that nobody had any very strong views about pricing and we could easily change the model.

The 80/20 Principle

Almost everyone has heard of the 80/20 Principle, but fewer than one in a hundred truly use it to its full potential. If you want to get this work done and produce significant improvements in performance, you will need to become its master.

Just to recap (you can find out more from one of Richard Koch's excellent books on the subject), in just about field of human activity 80% of effects arise from 20% of causes, and 80% of results arise from 20% of effort. So for example

- 20% of customers produce 80% of your profit

- A different 20% of customers produce 80% of your customer-related problems

- 20% of sales people make 80% of sales

- 20% of the information gives you 80% of the insight.

Turnaround specialists, who operate exclusively in areas where averagely competent people have failed, make extensive use of the principle. They never have more than three priorities. You may not be in a crisis, but I'd commend the same approach to you.

Here are some of the ways in which you can apply the 80/20 principle.

Only analyse 20% of what you could analyse. For instance,

don't calculate the profitability of every customer, or every product. Take a view on which will be in the top 10% and bottom 10%, and analyse those to validate your guess. If you can find some very profitable customers and some very unprofitable ones, then you are ready for action. Find more of the first, and eliminate or fix the second. Then, and only then, do you look at the rest of the portfolio, if you still need to. Identify those few actions which produce disproportionate results. Yes, you could start 10 initiatives, but you wouldn't complete any of them. Find the two or three most powerful levers, and concentrate your efforts on those.

Recognise that the 80/20 principle is very easy to understand and to master. Most people don't exploit it to anything like its full extent not because they fail to grasp it, or are too stupid to apply it, but because of psychological blocks.

These include:

- It feels lazy, and we are conditioned to work hard. It's true that lazy people make good use of the principle, but so do exceptionally effective ones.

- It feels too "broad-brush." You don't fully analyse anything. You do that 20% of the work needed to be sure that your conclusions are 80% right, and then take action. You may need to support your finance director through this one – they may well feel uncomfortable as their training and inclination tell them to do a "proper" job. You will need to explain that you don't need everything worked out to the last degree, and you can't afford to wait for it.

- It feels like "giving up". We get part way through a task, then stop. Recognise that once you reach a certain point, diminishing returns set in.

Think "Good Enough"

Remember what you are trying to do. As you look to learn new things about your business, you are not trying to build a case which will stand up to cross-examination in a court of law. You are not trying to write an article which would pass the peer-review process to be published in an academic journal. You are not trying to work things out to the same level of accuracy as you need in your annual accounts. You are operating to a lower standard of proof. You don't need to be accurate, and you don't need to be complete.

It doesn't matter if you only get part of the picture, so long as what you do see is useful.

Very rough estimates can be good enough. Let's say in half an hour you do a calculation which suggests that product A is attractive and product B is not. Suppose there are inaccuracies – product A might have been allocated 20% too little cost and product B 20% too much. Don't start collecting more data or doing more analysis until you have checked whether it would make a difference to your action. Very often it won't – even if the costs of product A and product B had been underestimated or overestimated by 20% it wouldn't change the fact that A is attractive and B is not.

Don't feel that you have to look at everything. You may have 100 customers but if you analyse 10 of them and find two really good ones and one horrible one you already have some actionable information. Before you do any more analysis, take some action. Make a plan for finding more customers like the very good ones, and for fixing the horrible one.

Getting Started

Use this matrix as a way of deciding where to start. Each of the following chapters offers suggestions for action. Anything you might try has a level of difficulty, and a level of impact. Take a moment to locate each action in the matrix to help you decide where to start.

Difficult		
Easy		
	Low Impact	*High Impact*

How to assess the impact? Chapter Six includes some pointers to help decide the likely impact of working on a particular area. Think hard about these, and put the different interventions in order of importance.

How to assess the difficulty? There are two things to consider here – how hard it is to do the analysis, and how hard it will be to motivate action once you have the results. Look at the method, and estimate how easy it will it will be in your organisation. Then, assess how difficult it will be to implement change based on what you find. Will you encounter resistance to the idea of dumping certain customers because they are unprofitable, or will there be a general feeling of relief once they have been shed?

Remember that hard analysis is still much easier than hard implementation. Look for areas where the right thing to do is not obvious; once you have uncovered it, actually doing it will be easier.

If at any time you need more help, turn to the last page.

When considering implementation, think carefully about the people who need to start doing different things to make things happen. A useful way to do this is AABB:

Audience – who are you talking to?

Action – what do they need to do, or do differently?

Benefits – what is the benefit – to them, not to you, not to the company – of doing things the new way?

Barriers – what might prevent them?

To take an example, suppose you determine that large customers are substantially more profitable than smaller, and that you have potential to sell more in that are. You therefore need salespeople to spend more time selling to large customers.

Audience   is it all salespeople, or just some? If some, who precisely?

Action   spend a greater proportion of time (specifically, how much?) working on larger accounts.

Benefits   to some extent, you determine these. They need to see how moving their attention to the larger accounts helps them make their quotas more easily, or enables them to earn more.

Barriers   what could these be? Maybe they will need to deal with more complex sales, involving multiple people in customer organisation. Or they may need to deal with more knowledgeable, more sophisticated buyers. Or maybe the sales cycle is longer, which means a lean few months before the higher revenues start to flow.

It might help to tabulate your thinking:

Employee group	Action	Benefit	Barrier	Difficulty H/M/L

The final column is an assessment of how it is going to be to sell the changes to each group.

Once you have been through the different areas and plotted them on the chart, proceed.

Chapter Two

The Problem-Solving Pyramid

*Problems Can Be Attacked From Many Directions, But Some
Directions Are More Fruitful Than Others.*

The first step in solving a problem is to understand where the cause is located, which can be at different levels in an organisation. For example, if you are worried about increased pricing pressure, giving your sales force negotiation training isn't going to help if you are trying to compete on price with the Chinese. This model is to help you be sure that you have located the real problem, and are not just dealing with a symptom.

The model uses a hierarchy of four levels. Generally, when a mistake is made about the location of the problem, it is usually put too low rather than too high. Interventions made at higher levels usually have greater impact. Problems at a higher level can make intervention at lower levels ineffective – for example, if a company's product is obsolete or too expensive, no amount of work on sales incentives or selling skills will produce an improvement.

The four levels are, in descending order:

- Strategy and Objectives: what is the product, who is the customer, who is the competition? How large is the company?

- Organisation: who is responsible for what? How is authority delegated through the organisation? Is this completely clear? Are there any overlaps or gaps?

- Incentives and information: what are the incentive arrangements (informal as well as formal)? Do they support the overall aims of the organisation? Is information available to show how well the organisation is progressing against its strategic goals?

- Individual performance: questions of skills and motivation.

You have to start at the top, and work downwards. There are two reasons for this. The first is that if you have a problem at a higher level, working at a lower level won't help. Suppose, for instance, that your problem is that sales are too low, and you decide that you need sales training, or negotiation skills training, for the sales force. There may be an opportunity to help them in those areas, but it won't do you any good if you are trying to sell the wrong type of product, or competing in areas where you don't have any competitive advantage.

Maybe you want negotiation training because you are struggling to get adequate prices from customers. If there is an incentive scheme in place based on achieving certain levels of volume, no amount of negotiation training will help you. If the easiest way for sales staff to meet their targets is to give way on pricing and "buy the business", then that is what they will do.

Perhaps the real opportunity is to increase sales by cross-selling; many customers only take part of the product range when they could take more. In this case, a frequent problem is poor information; it is hard to see who is buying what and therefore where the opportunities are. Increasing sales skill here is not likely to help until you have resolved the lack of information so that everyone can see what is happening.

Trying to solve the problem at too low a level is not merely ineffective, but creates stresses and strains in the organisation. Investing money in sales training could boost morale in the sales force, but not if your sales people return, newly fired up, to work and find themselves hampered by poor information or inappropriate organisation. Giving them training in negotiation so that they can achieve better prices while maintaining an incentive scheme which promotes volume will simply confuse them and risks creating cynicism.

Sometimes you may have a choice of which level to work at – things are not perfect anywhere, but neither are they disastrous. In this case there is a very good reason for starting at the top level; the higher you start the greater the leverage you obtain – greater impact for less effort.

With this in mind, let's take a look at the different levels, the typical issues that arise and how to deal with them.

Understanding When you Might Need to Upgrade Your Strategy

A huge amount has been written about "strategy," much of it by consultants or academics who would like you to believe that it is enormously complex, so that you need them to do it for you. Look behind this self-serving obfuscation, however, and "strategy" is very simple. It is just the "what," "who," and "why?" of the business – what do you sell, who do you sell it to, and why do they buy from you rather than someone else.

The final question, the "how" do we do these things, is the implementation of the strategy. If you have a coherent answer to "what", "who" and "why" you have a strategy. If what people actually do day to day is consistent with the answers you have given to the questions, you are implementing your strategy. If your strategy works in the market, and you implement it well, then you will be successful.

Strategy isn't as complex as the consultants and academics would have you believe, but it is fundamental. If your strategy is seriously wrong, no amount of operational excellence, motivation, efficiency, continuous improvement or anything else will save the business. With this in mind, here are some questions to help you determine whether you have a viable strategy:

Are you selling the right products? Clearly it is 100 years too late to be selling steam trains. If you are still in that market then even if you are the most efficient producer ever, selling the most technically advanced and highest quality steam trains the world has ever seen, you will not be successful. This is an extreme example, but there are many, many less obvious other examples of products that just can't be successful any more.

Are you competing with the right people, in the right market? Think of the rise of China. They are now a huge manufacturing power, and with their low costs very hard for western manufacturers to compete with. The manufacturers who do hold their own against Asian competition are those with a highly sophisticated, high-technology product. If you are not in that category, you will struggle.

Are you in the wrong part of the market? Look for example at the chocolate manufacturers Thorntons. For many years they were a premium brand, selling through their own stores. Then the market moved away from them. Other chocolate makers came in with more expensive, more glamorous offerings, which made Thorntons look rather ordinary. As one commentator put it "you might buy it as a present for your mother, but you wouldn't buy Thorntons to impress a girlfriend." Sales through the shops began to fall. To compensate, Thorntons increased sales to supermarkets. This created two problems. There was a marketing issue – it becomes harder and harder to maintain any idea of prestige or specialness about the brand when it is available in supermarkets at supermarket prices. There was also a financial issue – supermarkets buy at very low prices so that while sales held up, margins fell.

Are you the right size? Jack Welch famously confronted all GE businesses with the directive to "be Number One or Number Two in your market, or get out". There are many compelling reasons why businesses in the Number Three slot or below would struggle, however large they are in absolute terms. There is a minimum level of research and development spending needed to keep up to date. You can't spend less than your competitors in this area but if your sales are lower you are at a disadvantage. The same may well apply to sales networks or marketing spend.

For smaller businesses there may be an issue of skills mix. I did this exercise with a marketing consultancy. They needed a range of different skills to meet their clients' needs, and also needed a certain amount of depth, with senior people supported by more junior ones. It seemed that they could build a niche business with 10-15 people, or a full-service one with 45 or more (the strongest competitors had 80-plus). The issue for them was that they had 30 staff, and just enough business to support them. They either had to grow rapidly, a risky strategy, or become specialised.

One way to assess whether your strategy has a chance of being successful is to use Michael Porter's idea of the three generic strategies. Any successful strategy, he claims, is one of three types differentiated, lowest-cost or niche.

The differentiated strategy is based on being superior and in some way meaningful to the customer. This enables you to charge a higher price, which allows you to incur higher costs in producing your superior product or service. The questions to ask here are whether the differentiation you are claiming is recognised by the customer, and whether the extra price you can charge is enough to cover your extra costs.

Ask simply "why would a customer come to us when they could get something almost as good for a lower price from someone else?" If you can come up with a convincing answer, and see customers behaving in accordance with it, then you probably have a viable differentiation strategy.

The niche strategy is based on being more specialised than competitors. This lets you organise to be best at whatever specialised thing it is you do, because you don't have to worry about doing lots of other things. There are many different ways of being niche. You could work with many different types of client, but only do one very specific thing, like the law firm which only does "bet the company" work – matters which materially affect the client's future. You could work with only one type of customer, like the manufacturer of electrical connectors who specialises in very high reliability components for aerospace and military markets.

The third strategy, lowest-cost, can be superficially the most attractive but is in fact much more difficult than it looks. It has nothing to do with dropping prices to win business and then shaving costs here there and everywhere to maintain profits. A proper lowest- cost strategy is much more than that. It involves redesigning the whole business with a single focus on achieving the lowest costs in a way your competitors cannot emulate.

The best illustration of a successful lowest cost strategy is the low-cost airline. Everything the low cost airline does – the choice of airports it uses, the decision to use only one type of aeroplane, the decision not to transfer baggage from one flight to another – is based on its desire to minimise costs. A genuine lowest-cost strategy is hard. It requires a single-minded focus on minimising costs at the expense of just about anything else. It probably also requires you to be large, since economies of scale matter.

The alternative to having a viable strategy in line with one of the three generic models is, according to Porter, being "stuck in the middle". You have higher costs than the lowest-cost producer, but you are not sufficiently different or superior to justify a higher price. Or you may not be able to cover the whole market, but nowhere are you the most specialised.

It's worth pointing out that the biggest cause of poor strategy is not stupidity or lack of market insight or bad information, but simply the passage of time. Most bad strategies started as good strategies, otherwise the organisations suffering from them would never have reached the point they did. Markets change, new competitors enter, new products appear, all of which makes strategy formulation a continuous process. The question to ask is not "do we have a valid strategy?" but "how do we need to change our strategy to be sure that it continues to be valid?" or, even more starkly, "what is happening today that will invalidate our strategy and make us fail if we don't change it?"

The fact that good strategy becomes bad over time is not just the reason for bad strategy, but also the biggest barrier to changing it when it needs to be changed. To understand this, consider the story of Intel. Intel started as a manufacturer of memory chips, before developing into microprocessors. By 1984, when the processor business was still small, the memory business was in trouble. Japanese competitors were underselling Intel in memory chips. The strategic conclusion was obvious Intel had to abandon memory chips and bet the company on the newer processor business. Logically this was inescapable, but emotionally it was almost impossible to accept. Intel had been born as a memory chip business. After almost a year of "aimless wandering" of trying to fix the memory business, Andy Grove the president was having another agonised discussion with Chairman and CEO Gordon Moore.

Grove asked "If we got kicked out and the board brought in a new CEO, what would he do?" Moore replied without hesitation, "He would get us out of memories". So, asked Grove, "Why shouldn't you and I walk out the door, come back and do it ourselves?"

That is what they did, but it took more months of anguished discussion before they could convince the rest of the organisation and finally leave the memory business.

This gives you the real key to successful strategy – often you have to be willing to abandon what has made you successful in the past. The past, your achievements and the capabilities you have built up, are usually seen as a source of strength. Sometimes they can be your biggest threat.

You can see how this explains the story of Thorntons. They didn't get worse at what they were doing. Their chocolate was as good as it ever was, but the market moved around them. New competitors like Hotel Chocolat moved the market up, leaving Thorntons uncomfortably in the middle.

Strategy is easier than many of the gurus would have you believe, in one way at least. It is often quite easy to work out what you need to do. It probably takes less time and less work than you expect. On the other hand, strategy is harder than you expect when it comes to selling the necessary changes within the organisation. That can be hard, especially when you need to abandon what has made you successful in the past. There is no easy solution to this, but do at least help yourself by being clear as to what the argument is about. You will hear doubts about the data you have. You need to look in more detail at this, or that. Recognise this for what it is: the rationalisation of an emotional resistance, or of a fear of the future. Don't try to respond with more data, more reasoned argument. Engage with the emotion.

It's important to get the strategy at least approximately right before you try to improve or change other things. As is very clear from the examples, if there is something wrong with your choice of what you sell and who you sell it to, or you don't have a convincing story as to why customers buy from you rather than someone else, nothing you can do in other areas will help you much.

Assessing Organisation

Once the strategy is good enough – for now! – you can begin to consider other areas. Look next at organisation. Do you have the right people doing things the right way? For example, a children's book publisher sold substantial quantities through newsagents. They had a large team of merchandisers who visited shops to replenish displays, but this was no longer effective or economic. They realised instead that they needed to work with wholesalers who served the newsagents. These offered complete coverage, and so could visit more locations. They could afford to visit more often, as their representatives carried many more lines of products. The final step was to recruit a sales manager with experience of the sector who could recruit and manage the wholesalers.

I found a similar problem with the organisation of sales in one of my clients, an engineering company in Spain. They had many customers who received visits from sales representatives, but who did not place enough business to cover the cost of those visits. This business could never be profitable until they found a way to serve these smaller customers on the telephone or online.

Information and Incentives

After organisation, look next at the sort of incentives people receive, and the information they are given.

The questions are:

- Do incentives actually incentivise the behaviour we want?

- Does everyone have the information they need to know how well they are doing?

These seem very obvious questions, but very often the answer to one, or both, is unfortunately "No".

Some incentive schemes have no positive effect on performance at all, but it can be even worse. Sometimes, worryingly often, incentives can produce bad behaviour. In the chapter on pricing I mention the magazine publisher I came across, who had incentivised volume above all else in advertising sales. The sales force had done the logical thing and started discounting to make the sale and build volume. The end result had been advertising sold at 20% of what competitors were charging in similar publications.

If you want sales people to sell profitably, at a minimum you need to ensure that making unprofitable sales – chasing revenue, or "buying the business" – isn't rewarded. Also make sure that you provide the information people need to know whether they are getting it right or not. It's all very well, for example, telling sales people that they need to make profitable sales, not just any sales, but are you giving them good information on the profitability of their accounts? My researches over many different industries found that typically fewer than 10% of organisations have a really comprehensive set of reports in this area. Making customer or product profitability more visible can have dramatic results.

Case Study – the Power of Information

I had carried out a profitability study for a marketing consultancy. The results were typical, even if a little more extreme than usual. The average profitability of a contract was not too bad, but the average figure covered up some huge variations – remember the man who drowned while trying to cross a river with an average depth of four feet?

In particular, there was a group of projects which had soaked up one third of the total effort expended over the period and generated only 12% of the total profit. This was a huge drain – it equated to everyone in the firm working for a day and half a week almost for free.

What was also significant was that almost all of these low-profitability projects came from one of the three teams. This was odd, as this team had rather better clients than one of the others, who produced superior results. It was clear that the discrepancy came from the way the team sold or delivered its work. It seemed to me that these numbers were going to be quite embarrassing for David, the head of the underperforming team.

I wondered how I was going to present the results of the study, as I was expecting huge resistance from David. In the end, I decided to present the list of projects, in order of profitability, without comments. This I did, and waited for the explosion from David. It didn't come. He simply said "I see a lot of my projects at the bottom of the list. I need to do something about it," and he did. Over the next nine months the problem was resolved.

Skills and Motivation

Finally, once you are happy (that is happy enough, for the time being) with strategy, organisation, information and incentives, you can look at individual skills and motivation. The good news is that by this time some apparent skill deficits will have disappeared – the problems weren't caused by lack of skill or motivation, but by poor organisation or information, or inappropriate incentives. You are also in a much better position to start working on whatever issues of skill or motivation remain – you know what you need to do to support the strategy, you have the right information to guide and evaluate, and the incentives pull in the right direction.

Using the problem-solving pyramid is not a lengthy process. It prompts you to ask more questions, but once you have asked the right questions you usually realise that you know the answer already. A tiny amount of time invested at the start will pay huge dividends once you start to take action. The problem-solving pyramid will guide you towards the solution, offering maximum leverage. It will save you from the frustration which inevitably comes from trying to make changes at one level when the problem is at a higher level.

Digression – The Fundamental Attribution Error, or "That's Just the Way They Are"

How often have you heard someone (yourself?) decrying someone else's behaviour using terms like "they're greedy", "stupid", "selfish", "just downright bloody-minded...."

Stop. What you are hearing, or saying, is an example of

the Fundamental Attribution Error. What's that? It is the perfect example of social scientists' ability to come up with a really powerful, useful idea and then disguise it in impenetrable jargon. The basic idea is that we have an inbuilt tendency, when we see somebody else doing something we don't like, to explain it in terms of "that's how they are" rather than "that is what you would expect given the circumstances they are in".

Look at bankers, for example. Were they greedy and selfish? Or is the better explanation that they did pretty much what most people would have done in the same position? They had the opportunity to trade in securities they didn't understand, without any effective risk management (because nobody understood the risk). Everybody was telling them they were geniuses. They could earn huge bonuses if they were successful, without corresponding losses if they were unsuccessful. Given all this, wouldn't most people have done exactly what the bankers did?

Learning to spot when we are falling into the Fundamental Attribution Error and how to get ourselves out of it is hugely valuable, in fact liberating. Here is how. When you see someone doing something you don't like, ask yourself

- Under what system of incentives would this be rational behaviour?

- What would I do in their position?

- Do I see most people doing the same thing in this situation?

Being able to do this effectively turns an intractable problem, human nature, into a much more tractable one – designing organisations, systems and incentives which produce sensible behaviour. This is perhaps the most valuable application of the problem-solving pyramid it overcomes our natural bias to diagnose problems as being caused by individuals, and redirects our attention to other possible causes.

Case Study – Rapid Problem Diagnosis

At a meeting of a group of chief executives, one member asked "how do I get departmental managers to take more responsibility for controlling their departmental overhead cost?"

I had no idea – I knew nothing about his business. I could however help him work out the answer very quickly, using the pyramid. Go through the levels in order.

Strategy and Objectives: are all the managers clear on what is expected of them when it comes to control of costs? If asked, "Please tell me your understanding of what the company wants from you in terms of cost control," would they all give the same answer? Probably not.

Organisation: Is it clear which costs belong to whom? Are there any costs which don't have a clear owner, or where there is a joint responsibility? "No, it's all pretty unambiguous." Good.

Information: Do all the managers get good information – what the costs are, what they should be, why the variances arise? "Yes they do."

Move on to individual skills.

Do all the managers have the necessary financial skill to interpret the information they are given? "Hmm...some of them probably don't."

So there is the answer – reassert what's expected of the managers, and make sure all of them understand it. For those who need help, arrange a session with someone from the finance department to explain how to interpret and use the information they are given.

Action: next time to you want to solve a problem or make an improvement, run through the pyramid to be sure that you are acting in the right way.

Chapter Three

Management Accounts

...And Why You May As Well Throw Them Away

In managing performance, management accounts are often considered to be a vital tool. The fact is, though, that they are usually useless. In fact, you are lucky if they are just useless – they can be positively misleading. Here are some of the reasons why.

- They use unhelpful categories

- They don't say anything about the link between costs and revenues

• They are too aggregated

They tell us about what has happened, rather than giving us the information we need to predict what will happen.

Look, for example, at the marketing line in a typical set of management accounts. It's labelled "marketing costs," but doesn't in fact show more than a fraction of those costs. The salaries of those working on marketing are shown on another line – wages and salaries.

Once we separate out the marketing salaries and add them to the other marketing costs, we are still left with a whole list of unanswered questions. We spent this amount on marketing, but what did it actually produce? You would like to think that marketing helps us gain new customers, but what is the relationship between new customers acquired and marketing money spent? The management accounts don't even begin to address the question.

Let's suppose we can work out the number of new customers added by our marketing efforts. We spent £1m and gained 1,000 new customers. Is this good or bad?

There is nothing in the management accounts which helps us answer this question. We need the lifetime value of a customer – how much profit does a customer generate in a year, and how many years will they typically remain with us?

If the cost of acquiring a new customer is £1,000, so what?

If a customer generates £500 of profit in a year and stays for year, then we have lost money. If on the other hand a customer generates £1,500 of profit in a year and stays with us for three years, then we have made a very appealing return on investment. Given the lifetime value of a customer and the cost of acquiring one, we can determine where to spend our marketing budget. More than that, we can determine whether the business has a future or not – if it costs more to acquire customers than those customers are worth, then death is only a matter of time. How many sets of management accounts help us with this crucial calculation?

Management accounts have one useful function – they tell you whether things, in total, are developing in line with budget. They don't tell you

- if things aren't developing as planned, why the difference arises

- where you really make your money, and where you lose it (because everything is aggregated together)

- where you could spend less without hurting yourself, and where you could spend more and obtain a positive return on investment.

A large part of the problem with management accounts is that they are derived from the published financial accounts – accountants become very uncomfortable if the two things don't agree. The problem, though, is that the basic principles of financial accounts are positively inimical to producing information which might help you run the business.

Let me explain:

Financial accounts need to be consistent, both from year to year and between different companies. This is absolutely correct when it comes to reporting to investors on what the company's management has done with their money (the basic function of financial accounts). From a management point of view, however, consistency is not a virtue. Maybe this year you are particularly concerned with improving the profitability of customers, so your reporting needs to be organised around customers. Two years ago you were more interested in controlling overhead cost, so your reporting focused on that. In this case, inconsistency is a virtue.

Financial accounts have a completely different idea of accuracy. If you report a profit of £5m, the true figure had better be between £4.9m and £5.1m. Nobody ever heard of a company reporting its annual results as either excellent, acceptable or poor. This requirement for accuracy is in fact completely dysfunctional when applied to a profitability study. It takes forever, creates paralysis by analysis and often results in calculations so complicated that nobody understands them, nobody believes them and nobody does anything with them. If you are doing a study of customer profitability, it is quite adequate to divide all customers into three buckets:

- Excellent – we want more like these

- Acceptable – happy to have them and look after them, not worth huge effort to gain more similar

- Unacceptable – need to be fixed or dropped.

That's all that's needed. If you have determined that a particular customer offers excellent profitability, it doesn't matter whether it is twice as profitable as average, or five times. Stop analysing, and start looking for more similar ones.

Here are some ways to make management accounts more useful

Disaggregate

It's a pretty safe bet that whatever the management accounts are showing you, it's an average of many different things, and that average conceals some huge variations. If you have, for example, gross margin by product line, you can be sure that if you took any of those product lines and looked at the individual sales making them up you would find some with a margin twice the average and others with a margin half the average.

Similarly with marketing costs. Even once you have pulled all the marketing costs together (some recorded as salary, some as purchased costs) there is still much more to find out. You have an aggregate of marketing cost, but how much are you spending on different activities? How much, for instance, is aimed at selling more to existing customers, and how much at winning new customers? And then, how much do we gain from each of these?

Reorganise

There's nothing sacred about the categories of costs and revenues you use. Feel free to change them. If you report sales and cost of sales by product line, see what happens if instead you report them by customer.

Think about today's business versus yesterday's business versus tomorrow's business. Some parts of the business are past their best – products heading towards obsolescence, customers in declining industries, categories being taken over by new low-cost producers in emerging economies. This is yesterday's business. It probably still makes money, but it is in decline. Then there is today's business – profitable, successful. And then there is tomorrow's business – new products, or new types of customer. It's probably quite small, and represents a lot of work relative the money it makes. But it is the future. Looking at the time and effort going into yesterday, today and tomorrow can be revealing.

If you are looking at overhead costs, take a look at the costs not of departments, but of processes. You have costs in order processing (recorded probably as sales), in production scheduling (recorded in production), in despatch (recorded in warehousing), in invoicing (recorded in finance) and in credit control (finance again), but these are all just parts of one thing – the sales order and fulfilment process. Convention dictates that they be recorded in a range of different places so that we are prevented from getting a grip on them, but we need to overturn that convention if we are to discover anything useful.

Customise

What is bothering you, or exciting you, today? Do the numbers shed any light on it? If not, reorganise them until they do.

Use data to look forwards, not backwards

Most conventional reporting looks backward. It tells us where we have been, but not where we are going to go. The best it can offer us in this department is a trend which we can extrapolate (often an unwise idea, though).

However, data can tell us a huge amount about where we are going, if we simply use it intelligently. Here are some useful measures.

Measures for Products

Product Profitability

This is a fundamental. Every time I have done it, it has produced surprises. Some products are amazingly profitable while others, inevitably, are losing money. I know a private equity house which uses this as one of their basic techniques for improving performance, and they also find that the results are always surprising.

When you do it, make sure you take into account all the extra hidden costs that products tend to impose, but are hard to track. That is things like:

- Special packaging

- Emergency freight

- Pre-delivery samples

- Marketing support

- Customisation

- Unusual levels of returns or complaints

- Extended payment terms.

Product Half-Life

How long does it take for half your product range to become obsolete? At Intel, for example, 90% of December revenues come from products that weren't being sold in January. Your business probably doesn't have quite such a rapid cycle, but it's important to understand what it is. Estimate the half-life and compare that with your rate of new product introduction to see how effectively you are sustaining the business.

Profit by Life Stage

What proportion of your profit comes from:

- New products

- Products in early maturity (i.e. recently established)

- Products in late maturity (i.e. established for some while)

- Products in decline

This tells you what's going to happen, and how hard you need to work on innovation to maintain profits.

Profitability over the life cycle

How does the profitability of a product evolve over its life cycle? Does it improve, as you gain experience in production and buying the product becomes a habit with customers (so lower marketing costs)? Or does profitability decline, as competitors catch up and a distinctive new product becomes a commodity? This tells you many useful things about how to spend on innovation and marketing. How significant is the benefit of being first in the market? Do you spend your marketing money sustaining established products, or accelerating the launch of new ones?

Marketing Cost as Percentage of Sales/Profit

How effectively do you spend your sales and marketing budget? Look at the amount you spend on each of your product groups. Does it make sense? If a product is receiving a larger than normal amount of marketing cost, does it offer high potential? If another product seems to be neglected, is that right? Would it benefit from more? If you reallocated marketing spending, would total sales and profit rise or not?

Working Capital Requirements per Product

Some products may require much higher levels of working capital. They may sell to customers who take longer to pay, or they may require the company to keep higher levels of stock. For example, a manufacturer of alcoholic drinks saw vodka and scotch whisky as being equally attractive, as they cost the same to produce and sold for the same amount. When they took into account the stock levels, recognising that vodka could be sold immediately while whisky needed to be matured for at least three years, they realised the picture was quite different.

Measurements for Customers

Profitability by Customer

Anyone who has looked at this knows how surprising the results can be. Some customers are hugely profitable, while others are costing it money. Cable and Wireless the telephone operator discovered that 80% of its customers were unprofitable. A European logistics business found that one of its contracts with a major European manufacturer was costing it 20% of turnover.

Reasons may vary. Sometimes, customers may attach

greater or lesser value to the same product or service, and therefore pay more or less. At other times, it may that the company is better organised to serve a particular type of customer, which makes some types more profitable than others. Alternatively, there may be no inherent reason for differences in profitability, poor results simply being explained by inconsistent pricing or poor negotiation.

Working Capital Invested per Customer

A customer may pay more slowly than the average, which involves higher than average receivables. It may require non-standard raw materials or insist on deliveries at short notice, both of which involve higher than normal stock levels. These additional working capital levels, unless compensated for by higher margins, make these customers less attractive

Lifetime Value of a Customer

This is fundamental when it comes to planning marketing, and tells you a lot about the long term robustness of the company. Lifetime value is a function not just of revenue and profit per customer in a given year, but also of how long the customer will stay with you.

Cost of Acquiring a Customer

This is the cost, in marketing and selling, of acquiring new customers in a given period, divided by the number of new customers acquired.

Combined with knowledge of the lifetime value, this tells you what you need to know about your marketing spending. If the cost of acquiring a customer is less than the lifetime value, marketing is producing a positive return on investment. In fact, if the value of a new customer is significantly less than the cost of acquisition, it could be a prompt to spend more on marketing.

Following the trend of the cost of customer acquisition can give valuable information about market conditions. If the cost is increasing, the market is becoming more competitive and hence more difficult. Because most sales come from customers acquired in previous years, the effect of higher acquisition costs will be quite muted to begin with. That is why tracking them can provide such useful early warning.

Customer Turnover, or Churn

If you are in a subscription-based business like cable television or mobile phones, you spend a lot of time obsessing about this. If you are not in a subscription-based business, consider whether you give this measure the attention it deserves.

New customers probably cost a lot to acquire, and the

number of them in most markets is limited. An investment in reducing churn and hence increasing lifetime value, could give a better return than spending to acquire new customers.

Customer Profitability over Time

How does this evolve? Are longstanding customers more profitable than new ones, or does customer profitability decline over time? In either case, why? If there is no noticeable difference, does this have to be the case? What can you do to increase the profitability of a customer over time? In some industries this could be done by finding more efficient ways of serving a customer. In others it may be easier to increase the amount each customer purchases.

Customer Share of Wallet

Of al the money that your customer spends on things which you could provide, how much of it comes to you? Are you the sole supplier, the supplier of choice, or the second choice when the first choice supplier is out of stock? Or maybe you are just kept in play, given the occasional scrap in order to keep the main supplier on its toes?

It's important to think here about how to define the total market. If you are a full service bank then look at the customer's total spending on financial services. If your strategy for a particular market is to be niche provider of foreign exchange and treasury services, even if you could in theory offer loans, credit cards and all the rest, then your total market is FX and treasury.

Market Share

This is a tricky measure for two reasons defining "the market" can be surprisingly difficult, and chasing market share as an end in itself can be an excellent way of diluting profits.

Consider the definition of market share. What is BMW's market share? If it defines the market as "passenger cars", then it is tiny. If on the other hand, more sensibly, it defines its market as premium executive cars, then it is substantial. Or consider household detergent. Is "household detergent sold through supermarkets" a sensible definition of a market? At first sight yes, but wait. What do you do about brands such as Ecover, whose proposition if that they are much more environmentally friendly? Do they count as the same market? If they do not at present, might they in five years time? Is it plausible that, given current concern for the environment, the market for environmentally friendly products would converge with the "mainstream" market, or even take over the mainstream?

Rather than fixate on market share figures, ask about appropriate scale. If you did expand your sales, can you do it in a way that increases, or at least maintains, your profit and return on capital? If so, do it. On the other hand, you may well find that you are operating in some marginal markets which are diluting your returns. In that case, lower scale would be beneficial.

Don't assume that higher market share is inherently good. Test the assumption, and work out what sort of scale works best for you. After all, if you are achieving the best return on capital in the industry, who cares what market shares your competitors are achieving?

Identifying the Customer from Hell

Every business has them, and they exact a terrible toll in cost, staff morale and opportunity cost of other, better opportunities neglected while everyone struggles to deal with the problems that these customers present.

A comprehensive customer profitability analysis will find these people but there are simpler ways. Your staff know who they are, so you just need to ask customer service, technical support, operations, manufacturing, despatch... all will be able tell you who generates work disproportionate to the level of business being done.

Or just try this question: "It's 4.30 pm on Friday afternoon. The phone rings. It's a customer. Who do you least want it to be?"

Measurements for Marketing

Marketing as a Percentage of Sales

Fairly obvious, but consider two things:

- When you break the total down by product line or customer group, what do you see?

- How does it compare against what your competitors or peers are doing?

Looking at the breakdown of marketing by product or customer type, do the results suggest the optimal allocation of resources? Where the percentage is higher, is this justified by higher growth potential, or greater competition in that area? Are you allocating resources to opportunities, or to problems? That is to say, is your marketing developing new products or markets, or trying to sustain declining ones?

Funnel Statistics

What percentage of leads turn into prospects? What percentage of prospects turn into customers, and what are those customers worth? How do these figures differ across different markets or product types? What is the trend over time?

Cost of Gaining a New Customer

How much does it cost you in marketing for each new customer you add? Comparing this with the lifetime value of a customer gives you both a picture of the productivity of your marketing and the long term health of your business. If the value of a customer is large compared to the cost of acquisition, you could probably justify increasing your marketing spend in order to grow. If on the other hand the cost of acquiring a new customer is close to the lifetime value, particularly if the ratio is changing adversely over time, then you have a major problem approaching if you do not have a profitable way for the business to renew itself.

Measurements for Cash

Operating Cashflow as Percentage of Operating Profit

Over anything but the shortest period, this should average 100%. If it doesn't, then either:

- Creative accounting is going on (profit can be manipulated but cash cannot)

- The business is a cash trap: it produces an accounting profit but, because that profit needs to be constantly reinvested, it cannot be distributed.

Cash Invested by Business Segment

Take what you found out in the earlier section about profitability by product and customer, and relate it to the cash invested. Different segments may involve different levels of receivables, different levels of stock, or different levels of capital equipment.

Relate these different levels of capital employed to the different margins in the different sectors and you will find wide variations in return on investment. You may also discover something very significant about the cost of growth. If you plan to grow in segments which require higher than average levels of capital, you may find that your cash requirement rises far more than your sales. Beware!

CHAPTER FOUR

FINANCIAL ANALYSIS IN A HURRY

Avoiding Paralysis By Analysis

Why Paralysis by Analysis is a Problem

Paralysis by analysis is the largest cause of failure of profitability initiatives. To understand why that is, and how to avoid it, we need to look at the organisational and psychological dynamics. The first and most obvious problem is that if the work takes too long to do it won't get done, but there is more to it than that.

Excessive complexity doesn't just make the whole process longer, but also makes it harder to explain and sell the results to the rest of the organisation. Don't underestimate the importance of this. It's not unusual that 20% of the time spent on a project like this is spent doing the analysis and developing the conclusions, while 80% is spent, one way or another, selling the conclusions to the organisation. Give yourself a chance of success and make sure that the conclusions are easy to sell – make sure that they can be explained simply to people who don't have a numerate background, and may often be biased against the sort of action that the results imply.

Be prepared for people to challenge the conclusions. They may simply be surprised at the results, and therefore find them hard to believe. Or they may believe them very well, but not like the conclusions drawn from them. In either case, make sure your work is robust. If you have asked people to give you estimates of various things, be sure that there is a clear trail from your conclusions back to the data they gave you.

Don't get drawn into discussions about whether your work is absolutely correct. It isn't – some things have been estimated, and there will be small errors in places. Take the line "of course there are inaccuracies, but if we corrected the issues you point out, would it change the overall picture? Would it change what we need to do?"

Maintaining momentum is crucial. The risk of paralysis increases exponentially with the time elapsed since the work last produced an actionable conclusion. Partly this is practical – the longer you go without coming up with something useful, the more likely it is that some crisis will blow up to distract attention and divert resources elsewhere. Partly it's psychological – the longer we have to wait for something interesting, the less likely we are stick with it. It would be like a film in which nothing happens in the first 20 minutes, or a detective novel where we reach page 100 before anyone gets murdered. Design your project to make sure that something useful comes out as soon as possible. Don't aim for the most important finding, aim for the quickest. Publish results as you get them, don't wait until you have the complete picture.

Measurement by What?

This is absolutely fundamental to the correct analysis of results, but it can be quite hard to grasp. The point is that it is misleading to allocate costs in line with revenue, as is so often done. We need a more realistic way of allocating costs, and that is according to the relevant "transaction." The correct transaction depends on the nature of the business, and this is where it becomes difficult. There are a couple of ways I have used to determine the right basis of analysis.

Trial and error: The aim is to find a way of analysing the business – by product, by customer, by manufacturing process – which makes different parts of it look different. '

your first attempt doesn't product an interesting result, try cutting the data in some different way. As an example, I did a project with an engineering company. It had around 700 customers, several thousand product lines in three main product groups. I looked first at the products, but this was not helpful they all showed similar margins. So I then looked at customers, and this was extremely revealing. Allocating the cost of sales visits and order processing to each of the customers showed that they had very different profitability. This provided the key to the project there was a need to find a more cost-effective way of serving small customers, and to direct efforts towards gaining more customers like the highly profitable ones.

Identify the Limiting Factor: Each business has a limiting factor. What is the factor which would first constrain growth? In a consulting business it may be availability of staff with the appropriate skills. In a retail bank, it is probably the number of customers. (It is difficult to persuade customers to change banks, and much easier to sell additional services to existing customers). In a business that uses large capital equipment – chemicals, printing, injection moulding, airlines – the limiting factor is the capacity of that ˥l equipment.

ˑve identified the limiting factor, then analysing that basis – money made by hour of professional time spent, by customer in the bank, by plant or element of plant or airline seat – is usually highly revealing.

Shortcuts

First Shortcut – Start with the Decisions

In an ideal world, we would create a comprehensive dataset which could then be analysed to illuminate any decision. In practice, this is rarely possible. By first establishing our range of options, we can limit the work to only those areas which are relevant to the decisions we might take.

Second Shortcut – Be Hypothesis-Driven

This means that rather than using figures to reach conclusions, we produce some hypotheses and limit our analysis to that which will confirm or deny the hypotheses.

Hypotheses can come from a variety of different sources:

- Strategic: it is reasonable to suppose that products or services where we are perceived as unique, and important to our customers, will be highly profitable. Conversely, if we are providing services which can be provided from India, say, then unless there is something exceptional about them they are unlikely to be attractive.

- Knowledge of other organisations.

- Competences: things which make use of well-developed and distinctive core competences are likely to be more profitable than things which others can do better.

Third Shortcut – Focus on Incremental Costs Only

It is easy to spend a long time allocating items of overhead such as office rent, management salaries and all the costs involved in hosting data. Usually, however, these costs will not change significantly under any decisions unless the changes planned are really fundamental. They can therefore be left alone, and time spent only on those costs which would be saved if an activity were eliminated, or increased if an activity were added.

Fourth Shortcut – Set a High Level of Materiality

The usual standard of accuracy applied to annual and monthly accounts is almost certainly far too high for this purpose. Differences between profitable and unprofitable activities tend to be quite gross. It is almost never a question of debating whether a particular activity generates 45% or 55% margin – it usually comes down to the difference between 20% and 70%. It is not necessary to rank everything in order. It is enough to put any activity, product or customer into the right one of three buckets:

- Excellent – search for more of these

- Acceptable

- Unacceptable – fix or terminate

It makes sense to do a preliminary, very rough, analysis, on one page if possible. Then see how robust the conclusions are. Usually, the conclusions will not change even if the most profitable areas have their costs understated by 25% and the least profitable have their costs overstated by the same amount.

Usually, the very rough analysis will be robust in most areas, and only a few will require further work to refine them.

CHAPTER FIVE

APPLYING SYSTEMS THINKING

That's just management-speak for
"recognising that everything is connected"

Start with an example:

Case Study

A software company had severe, longstanding problems collecting receivables. From time to time they would apply a burst of energy and achieve a temporary improvement, but it was never long until the situation lapsed back to the usual.

Some very difficult discussions with the bank had brought this issue to the chief executive's attention. His view was that collecting receivables was the finance department's job, and they needed to get on with it. More calls, more aggression, more activity. The problem was, that this was exactly what they had been trying for years, and the results never seemed to last.

I did something very obvious, but which had never been done before. I went through all the overdue amounts to find out what the problem was and who in the company could resolve it.

It turned out that 85% by value of the problems were in one of these three categories:

Software doesn't perform in accordance with documentation
The customer is saying "it doesn't do what it says on the tin. The Omgeo gadget doesn't interface properly with the FX gizmo." Nobody in finance even knew what this meant – it needed the software developers to resolve it.

Quality of professional services
The customer is saying something like "I know Fred was on site for 20 days last month, but he didn't know what he was doing. I'm not paying for more than 10 days." Finance can't resolve this either – the professional services people need to get involved.

Contractual confusion

The customer has five separate maintenance contracts for different parts of the system, signed at different times. Each involves an annual maintenance charge. We have sent one invoice for the whole lot, and the customer can't reconcile the total amount to the five contracts. We need to speak to the legal department who deal with contracts.

What do these issues have in common? None of them can be resolved by the finance department, the people tasked with collecting the money.

Once we developed a system for identifying who needed to take action, and making that they knew what they needed to do, the problem was rapidly resolved, and stayed resolved.

The moral of the story? If an apparently simple problem has resisted the obvious solution for any length of time, it's probably because you defined it too narrowly. You are assuming that the problem is located in, and can be solved in, one department or function when in fact you need to step back and look at the at a larger picture.

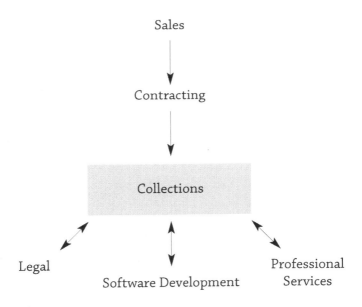

Insoluble Problem

Collections

Soluble Problem

Sales

↓

Contracting

↓

Collections

Legal ↔ ↑ Software Development ↕ Professional Services

Think about some of the interconnections you will have to deal with:

Cash vs Profit

This is so important that there is a whole chapter on it later. There are lots of ways of boosting profit by damaging cashflow. Avoid them.

Front Office vs Back Office

One popular idea when times get tough is to declare war on "unproductive" back office costs. This rather misses the point that back offices and support functions do necessary work. Salespeople need to do administration, or have it done. The Chief Executive needs to design PowerPoint presentations. The Finance Director needs to maintain files of all sorts of things. You can't eliminate back office and support functions – all you can do is move them to people who cost more, don't do them so well and have more difficult things to do.

Sales vs Production

You can try to make more sales by being more flexible, offering lower quantities, doing more customisation, offering shorter lead times. This may be exactly the right thing to do, but do you know what the impact is on production? Can you track the costs involved? Are you putting a proper price on this better service? In sum, is it making you any money, or costing you?

This is an area where you become dramatically better simply by deciding to. Whenever you look at an area or function, stop to think about the interconnections.

- Action: when you want to solve a problem or make an improvement in a particular area, draw a map like the one above showing all that areas interconnections.

CHAPTER SIX

GETTING DOWN TO WORK

...In the Right Order

We have dealt with tools. Now it's time to start work. The next few chapters look at different areas in which you can act to improve financial performance. The order in which I have written them is deliberate – it represents what in my experience is the best order to tackle them.

You won't necessarily want to go through the steps in the same order, but here's my logic. Use it as a starting point.

Begin by dealing with cashflow. Almost everyone should start here. Cashflow is the truly essential thing. If you are losing money but still, somehow or other, generating cash, then you time to resolve all your other problems. If on the other hand you run out of cash then you are finished, regardless of what profit you may be reporting.

After cashflow, I suggest that you look at pricing. As explained in Chapter Six, this is the area in which there are often the largest gains to be had, and it is also the area where little attention may have been paid. Making changes here also tends to be relatively easy.

Next, see which unprofitable customers or products you suffer, and deal with them. You need to be confident about your pricing before you do this – after all, you don't want to drop an unprofitable product which could be improved by being priced better. Work at this stage is relatively easy – identify the most profitable activities, give them priority and remove or resolve the profitability drags.

This done, you are in a position to identify any surplus capacity, and if necessary remove it.

Finally, you arrive at the issue of efficiency, eliminating waste. There are two good reasons for leaving this to last. It's likely to be the hardest, and you need to know what the business will look like before you do it. After all, your basic technique for eliminating excess cost will be to assess whether it serves any purpose. For that, you need to know what you are trying to do.

Setting Your Own Priorities

If you are not convinced that this is the right order for you, or you would just like to make sure, here are some ways to check.

Remember that you are not looking for the action that will make the greatest impact. You are looking for the action that makes the greatest impact relative to the amount of effort required. Suppose you have a choice:

• Plan A – takes ten hours, makes £10,000

• Plan B – takes 200 hours, makes £100,000.

Do A first. Then, and only then, look at B.

To help you clarify your ideas, use the impact and difficulty matrix from Chapter One. Here is a typical one based on experience, but you need one specifically for your situation.

Difficult	_Raise Efficiency_	_Cut surplus capacity_
Easy		_Pricing_ _Cut unprofitable_ _activity_
	Low Impact	_High Impact_

Let's think about how you would assess the impact. For each of the areas on which we could work, there are characteristics of the business which give us a clue as to its potential. Here they are for each of the areas:

Cash

Indicating High Potential	Indicating Low Potential
Service Business	Product Business, retail business
Recurring service (such as a maintenance contract or retainer)	One-off service
Business carries stock of raw material or finished goods	Business does not carry stock
Larger corporate customers	Customers are owner-managed businesses or private individuals

Pricing

Indicating High Potential	Indicating Low Potential
Unique or differentiated product	Commodity product
High gross margin	Low gross margin
Range of different customers with different value preferences	Small number of customers, or all customers essentially the same

Understanding Customer and Product Profitability

Indicating High Potential	*Indicating Low Potential*
Customised product or service	Standardised product or service
Customers have range of special requirements – customisation, special packaging, marketing support	Customers receive essentially the same product or service
Range of different customers, with different uses and different ideas about value	Customers essentially very similar
High value-added, i.e. substantial costs accounted for by internal resources not purchased	Low value added – small margins over purchased costs
Wide range of different products or services	Narrow range of products or services
Different products or services produced from same, shared resources (people or machines)	Each product or service line produced by dedicated resources
Larger amount of cost associated with serving customers (selling, account management or after-sales service)	Small amount of cost involved in serving customers

Eliminating Spare Capacity

Indicating High Potential	*Indicating Low Potential*
High proportion of costs are fixed (permanent staff or capital equipment)	Low proportion of costs are fixed (purchased inputs or subcontractors)

How Difficult Would it Be?

Once we have idea of the likely impact of working in the different areas, we need to assess how difficult it is likely to be. Here are the factors to consider:

What information do we need? In some areas this might be considerable. Understanding customer profitability, for example, need not be as daunting as it first appears, but is going to take an amount of work. Changing the basis of pricing, on the other hand, may not take much research. Simply looking at what you doing in the light of different principles can often produce new ideas, which you can test by experiment.

How many people are involved? Change involving large numbers of people will be harder, and slower, than something that needs to involve just a few. It's also vital to consider how receptive people are likely to be. Change initiatives that involve selling a difficult message to a large unreceptive audience don't have a great record of success. If you subscribe to a heroic paradigm of management you may be unconsciously drawn to these, but try to be a pragmatist. Your job is to obtain the greatest impact with the smallest effort.

Are you taking decisions, or changing behaviour? Consider making a change to pricing policies. Do you just need to change the price list, a decision? Or do you need to change the behaviour of all the sales people who are out there doing deals? Different organisations have different strengths and weaknesses, but generally speaking making decisions which can be straightforwardly implemented is going to be easier than whole scale behaviour change.

Where in the problem-solving pyramid do we need to act? Remember that the higher up you act, the greater the impact.

How much control do we have in this area? If we have strong controls already – like a price list which everyone observes – it will be easier to change than if we have a situation where everyone is accustomed to doing what they want with limited control from outside.

How risky is it? Or, more pragmatically, what could go wrong? Are there things you don't know that could hurt you? For example, raising prices generally carries some risk. Introducing a new higher-priced option alongside the existing offering should be low risk the worst that can happen is that nobody takes it which, if you haven't invested too much in developing it, is no big deal.

Once it's done, the way ahead is clear. Start on the easy, high impact actions, then look at high impact but more difficult or lower impact but easy. Ignore the difficult low impact ones – the ones you would probably have started with if you hadn't worked through the process in this book.

CHAPTER SEVEN

CASH

...and Why it's Usually Not King

"Cash is King", the saying goes. If that's true, then sometimes cash is like King Umberto II of Italy, who ruled for little more than a month in 1946 before being exiled. In 1947, the Italian constitution barred him and his male heirs from ever setting foot in Italy again.

We'll get to the practical techniques for managing cash, but first let's understand why those techniques, which are about as far from rocket science as it's possible to get in business, seem to be so inconsistently applied. There are things that you have to do before you can start applying the techniques.

It's a Trade-Off

Remember the old saying "good, cheap, fast – choose any two?" If you want a good job done fast, it won't be cheap. If you want a good job done cheaply, it won't be fast.

There is a similar trade-off between revenue, profit and cash. If you want to maximise sales without affecting profit, one popular way to do it is to sweeten the deal with longer payment terms. Or maybe you hold higher stocks to make sure that you never lose a sale because an item is out of stock. Both of these expedients have no effect on the profit and loss account but damage your cashflow. Similarly, if you want to improve your margins, you can probably reduce costs by buying in larger quantities, or manufacturing in longer runs. Again, the impact on the profit and loss account is wholly and visibly positive, but the effect on your cashflow is negative and largely hidden.

The Problem with Trade-Offs

The way many trade-offs are handled is: for people not to notice them, deny that they are necessary, believe that they can have the best of both worlds, or just decide to ignore the whole issue. The result is that tradeoffs are made by default or by accident, without any consideration of what's best for the organisation

Once you have identified that this is the source of the problem, it's not hard to see how to deal with it.

Trade-offs are made at the da
each time a sale is made or a p
production run planned. They a
level, in the overall design of the l

Trade-offs at the Operational Level

It's not that difficult to see when you are making a trade-off. Any time you do anything that has an impact on revenue or profit, identify the cash impact as well. There are many, many areas, for example:

- length of payment terms to customers

- stock levels set to ensure continuity of production or supply

- purchase quantities decided to minimise unit costs

- production runs set to maximise efficiency, at the cost of high stock levels.

Dealing with Cash Trade-offs at the Strategic Level

The traditional business planning or budgeting process works like this:

- first, set the level of revenues

d, massage the costs to produce an acceptable
rofit

- third, (and a pretty poor third, at that) work out the
  cash requirements and assume that they can be
  met.

Think about all the business plan or budget meetings you
have ever been in, and the percentage of time spent on
revenues or profits. Has it ever been less than 90%? That
doesn't leave much time to look at cash.

Reverse the process. Start with cash. How much cash do
you have? What can you do with it? The answer to the second
question is always "more than you first thought."

Apply the same level of intensity, ingenuity and creativity
to economising on cash as you do to minimising costs and
you will be surprised at what you can achieve.

How to Think More Intelligently About Cash

The first thing we need is a way of thinking about the tradeoffs
we make between profit and cash. If a supplier offers lower
prices in return for ordering in larger quantities, and therefore
tying more cash up in stock, how do we decide whether the
offer is worth accepting or not? Use the concept of velocity –
specifically, the velocity with which sales turn into cash.

Let's illustrate with an example. A producer of alcoholic drinks made both vodka and scotch whisky. Both cost about the same to make, and sold for the same amount. They therefore assumed that the two products were equally attractive. Until, that was, somebody pointed out the difference in velocity. Vodka, once distilled, is shipped direct to the wholesaler or retailer, invoiced and the cash received within weeks. Scotch, on the other hand, has to be kept in a bonded warehouse for at least three years before being sold. It produces the same revenues per case, the same profit margin, as the vodka but you have to wait three years longer for it. Now it's obvious that, other things being equal, vodka is a more attractive product. If the distiller has the opportunity to invest in growing sales of vodka or scotch, and the same effort in either area would produce the same result, it clearly makes sense, from a cash point of view, to concentrate on the vodka. Conversely, suppose that they made a big push to sell more scotch, and were successful. That success could kill them – they would need enough cash to make large quantities of whisky, but not receive it back for three years. If it's going to be as attractive a product as vodka, scotch needs to offer substantially higher margins to compensate for the lower velocity.

We can develop this idea of velocity to cover cases wh the differences between products are not so huge, a margins are different.

Imagine two products. Both sell 1,000 units per month, cost £1 to buy and sell for £2. The only difference is that we can buy product A in quantities of 1,000, while the minimum order quantity for product B is 2,000.

Product A has velocity of 12, because 12 times a year we sell all our stock and get paid. Product B, on the other hand, has velocity of 6 because it takes two months to sell out the stock, so we can go through the cycle of paying cash out for stock and receiving it back for sales only six times in a year.

The profit margin in both cases is 50%. The return on investment is margin times velocity, so:

- Return on investment for product A = 50% x 12 = 6

- Return on investment for product B = 50% x 6 = 3

This gives us what we need to evaluate the return on investment of any product, based on the margin and the velocity. If the availability of cash is constraining our growth, it shows us where to focus our efforts to grow with the
~f cash. When we need to make tradeoffs
cash requirements, it tells us the

more useful way to use the idea of grasped the concept, we can go through the whole business and work on increasing its velocity, with dramatic results.

Accelerating Cashflow

To accelerate cashflow through the business, start off with a view of the whole process. This is a general view; not all businesses will have all stages.

- Buy raw materials or products for sale

- Keep raw materials or products for sale in stock

- Convert raw materials into finished products

- Keep finished products in stock

- Sell finished products

- Invoice sales

- Get paid for sales

At each of these points there are ways to increase velocity. Let's look at them in order.

When it comes to buying raw material or finished product,

what can we do? We can talk to suppliers about things other than price. What is the minimum economic order quantity? If the supplier will give us sensible prices for smaller orders, then we can hold less stock. The less we hold, the greater the stock velocity, or turnover.

We also need to talk to the supplier about reliability – if we are going to hold smaller stocks and replenish more frequently, we need to be sure that the supplier will supply when required. We should also think about where the supplier is located – Chinese suppliers offer very good prices, but long lead times. Observation of my own clients suggests that stock velocity for goods from China is one third of that for goods sourced closer to home. The extra margin from low prices needs to be very appealing to make up for this.

Once we have raw materials in stock, we need to convert them into finished goods. Here the question is how we plan production. Do we make in long production runs, which mean efficiency, or shorter runs more closely matched to demand? The first will offer better margins, but lower velocity as the finished goods will stay in stock longer.

Once the finished product has been made, and possibly held in stock for a while, we sell it. Very often this is seen as the end of the process, but it isn't. The process doesn't end until we get paid. Simply repeating this basic fact again and again until everybody remembers it can make a huge difference. Increasing velocity at this stage is a matter of invoicing promptly (don't wait until the end of the month!) avoiding queries (sending invoices that everyone can understand) and dealing rapidly with any problems that do arise (making sure that everyone understands how important it is to get paid on time, and what their role is in making sure that it happens.) That's about it for a manufacturing business, or a business which sells things, but in a service business there are many, many more exciting possibilities.

Think carefully about contract terms, and when you are able to invoice. Don't automatically assume that you need to wait until the work has been done to invoice it. There are particular opportunities with regular services.

A firm of accountants working with small businesses, for example, prepares monthly accounts and also does the year end accounts and returns. Two thirds of the work is in the monthly accounts, while the other third is done at the end of the year. However, it doesn't wait until the end of the year to invoice the work – it invoices the same each month, so that by the end of the year one third of the year's fee is in the bank for work which has not yet been done. Clients don't generally object to this – even if they have a general idea t something in advance, a regular mont plan. In any case, the effect on any one though the total effect on the accounti

Don't allow payments to depend on completing a project. Most projects don't end neatly – they reach a point of 99% completion with only a few small things remaining to be done. It may take weeks or months to finish the remaining 1%, and you do not want to be waiting for any substantial amount of money at this point. Aim for a payment schedule which is at least in line with work being done, preferably ahead of it.

Ask for payment in advance. You may well be surprised by how easily clients agree. This is particularly true if you are dealing with large companies. There are some things very useful to know about buyers in large companies:

- They are generally held to account for costs, not cashflow, so they don't much mind when in the accounting year they pay

- If they are on good terms with their accounting department, they have mechanisms for spending money in one year and accounting for it in the next (it's called the prepayment)

- They care deeply about keeping costs in line with budget – and this means not too low, as well as not too igh.

Understanding exactly where your buyer is against their budget is very, very helpful. Remember that they don't want to underspend any more than they want to overspend. This means, particularly towards the end of the financial year, that they may be positively looking for ways to spend more money. If they don't spend it by the end of the year they lose it, and may even have next year's allocation reduced (after all, if you didn't spend all the money this year, why would you need it next?).

The other thing about large corporate buyers is that they always worry that their budgets will get cut part way through the year, if revenues start to fall below target. The best way to avoid this is to spend the money as soon as possible in the year, even if the work isn't done until later.

When I was commercial director of a marketing consultancy, we took full advantage of all of this. We would routinely ask for 50% of the fee on signature of contract, and mostly get it. Very rarely did we have to settle for less than a third.

The finance department produced a monthly report showing the amount of work we had done on each project compared to the amount of work we had done. There was a very clear expectation that any work done would be more than covered by invoices issued and in the rare cases that that wasn't the case the account manager would be asked firmly to raise an invoice.

Towards the end of year we would remind all the account managers to ask their clients if they had any budget to use up. If they had, we would help them out with an invoice in advance of next year's work. One year, we had a request from a major client for an invoice for £200,000. "Just put something vague on it," they said, "and we can decide next year what we want you do for the money. All that matters for now is that the invoice be in the finance department before Christmas".

It is not exaggerating to say that the combined effect of all these cashflow tricks was to transform the company's position. We started it with a bank overdraft but soon paid that back. We built the company on customers' money – at one point we had the equivalent of four months' revenue in the bank for work we had not yet done.

Look for creative options for financing your customers. Here are some examples:

A supplier of printing supplies diversified into supplying printing presses. It could make sales, but only by financing its customers. This put a severe strain on its balance sheet as it was having to buy and pay for expensive equipment but wait several years to be paid. The solution was highly creative. It sold the presses at much reduced prices, with an agreement that the customers would buy an agreed minimum quantity of consumables at enhanced prices which paid for the press. With this, the supplier went to a bank who agreed to lend the money for it to buy the presses, to be paid back out of the extra margin on the supplies.

You might ask why the supplier couldn't just broker finance arrangements whereby a bank or finance house lent money to the customers, but I suspect that the real reason could be seen in the customers' balance sheets. Although the customers have in effect committed themselves to a series of future payments (the extra cost of the consumables) in exchange for acquiring a capital asset (the press), just as they would had they taken a loan or entered into a leasing agreement, with this arrangement they don't need to show any loan or long term obligation on the balance sheet. For a financially hard-pressed printer, this may be the most important thing of all.

There may be other, less convoluted arrangements available. I once spoke to someone who was planning to open a private members' club. He was planning to charge membership fees monthly, and didn't think that prospective members would pay for a full year. I pointed out that there are finance houses which specialise in this situation, th
pay the club for a year's subscription
monthly. This completely changed
reducing the amount of money he
investors. It's worth mentioning tha

because my wife was a member of a health club which did it, which shows that it's worth paying attention to what's going on around you – you never know when it might come in useful.

The (Often Malign) Power of Incentives

Incentives are often a big part of the problem. Take two examples:

1. Salespeople have to make sales. The level of discounts is carefully controlled, but the length of payment terms may not be. I came across one software company where payment schedules for new licences could stretch out three years into the future. The revenues were reported in full when the contract was signed, so the horrible effect on cashflow was very well hidden.

2. Buyers need to keep items in stock. This means that they need to be in constant dialogue with sales to get the latest forecasts, and able to call on the goodwill of suppliers when they are caught short. Alternatively, they can just maintain huge stocks. This is what happened in the case study which follows.

Case Study

Reviewing the purchasing function in a manufacturing company, I found the purchasing manager about to place an order for four years' worth of one item. I asked why, particularly when the company was desperately short of cash.

To me it seemed an insane decision, but the purchasing manager was acting entirely rationally. Her objectives were to ensure that everything was in stock at all time, and achieve the lowest possible unit cost, which in practice meant ordering from China. The fact that the Chinese supplier imposed a high minimum order quantity on this slow-selling item wasn't considered.

You can't criticise middle managers for doing what they're told to do even if, as in this case, it was pushing the company to the brink of insolvency.

Education, not Control

How do organisations get people to do what they want? Usually it's by incentives and control. Reward them when they do what they are supposed to, try to prevent them doing the wrong thing, and whack them if they do break the rules. The famous behavioural psychologist B F Skinner found that this worked really well for conditioning behaviour in pigeons, and Pavlov had a lot of success with dogs, but you have to query whether the approach works well with humans, especially when you are asking people not simply to maximise one variable, but to make sophisticated tradeoffs between several variables.

Think instead about educating people. Help them see beyond their own area, be sure they understand what senior management is trying to do, show them how their behaviour impacts on the results of other departments'.

Think about sharing information. If everyone is responsible for managing the trade-offs between revenue, profit and cash, everyone needs to know what these are. If your finance director spends time obsessing about this issue (as they should!), that thinking needs to be shared. How much information do you share?

Traditionally in many companies cash hasn't been managed with even a fraction of the intensity applied to revenue and profit. Until two years ago, this wasn't a problem – capital was cheap and plentiful. That's no longer the case, and thinking needs to change.

So there you have the answer. To manage cash, educate everyone about it.

For the sales people – make them conscious of the effect of any extended terms. Give them a policy of when to offer extended terms, and what they have to get in return.

For the purchasing department – think about the

tradeoffs between getting the lowest possible cost, and maintaining sensible stock levels.

For the finance department – make them the standard-bearers for thinking about cash. There's not that much that they can do on their own, but they can educate everyone else, and let them know how they are doing.

Action: make sure everyone in the organisation understands the importance of cashflow, and how what they do affects it.

Doing the Work

Go through the whole sales and production cycle of the business, and set out all the stages.

It will probably look something like this:

- Sales forecasting

- Production planning

- Materials purchasing

- Manufacturing

- Sales

- Delivery

- Invoicing

- Cash collection

You may have additional steps or, as for example in a service business, some elements may not be there, or happen in a different order.

Once you have identified all the steps, for each one, document four things:

- Who takes decisions that impact on cashflow?

- What incentives operate that might make them favour profit margin over cash, or vice versa?

- What tradeoffs they have to make between profit and cashflow?

- What do they need from people in other parts of the company, in terms of information and cooperation, to make the best decisions and produce the best result?

Example One:

The Purchasing Manager in a Manufacturing Company:

Takes decisions on whether to order earlier in large quantities, or later in small quantities.

Has an incentive to achieve the minimum possible lowest cost and always to maintain stock.

Minimising unit cost and avoiding stock-outs naturally leads to ordering in large quantities, well in advance of forecast requirements, which leads to poorer cashflow – a longer delay between paying for materials and receiving payment for finished goods.

She relies on a manufacturing plan which tells here what will be needed by when, which in turn depends on a sales forecast. The less confident she is about the accuracy of these, the more she will tend to order and the worse cashflow will become.

Now the position is clear, and you look for opportunities to:

- Change incentives to give greater weight to cashflow

- Provide better information to help people achieve the best result

- Improve communication and cooperation between different areas.

Potential Pitfalls

The most important point to watch is to be sure that incentives change in reality as well as on paper. The purchasing manager in the example above would need permission to pay higher unit costs and occasionally be out of stock in the interests of reducing the amount of cash tied up in stock.

You may also need a change in approach to the way you set targets, away from bargaining towards genuine collaboration. Very often individuals' objectives are set by negotiation, in which the employee tries to get the bar set as low as possible, the employer tries to get it set as high as possible and n either side shows what they genuinely believe is possible. This can work up to a point when it's a matter of maximising or minimising one variable, but it's much less effective when trying to arrive at the best tradeoff between several variables. It may help to tabulate the results, as in this example:

Person	What they do	Interfaces – information used, interactions with others	Incentives – positive and negative	Effectiveness (current)	How hard to change?
Purchasing manager	Plan purchases – determine investment in stock	Sales forecast. Communicates with sales and manufacturing	Minimise stockouts mimimise unit cost – not helpful in conserving cash	Low – focused on other objectives	High to medium – educate, adjust incentives

Chapter Eight

Pricing

Usually The Major Missed Opportunity

For many businesses, work on pricing offers the single fastest, lowest risk and most powerful way of improving profitability. McKinsey & Co studied the cost structure of 1,200 companies and found that, typically,

- 1% increase in average price produced an 11% increase in operating profit

- 1% increase in sales volume produced a 3.7% increase in operating profit

- 1% reduction in fixed costs produced a 2.7% increase in operating profit.

Remember also that these figures apply in reverse – give away an average 1% on price and you are sacrificing 11% of operating profit.

Here's an interesting question: in your organisation, who would be more likely to be criticised, a salesman who consistently gave away 1% of the price, or a departmental manager who overspent her budget by 5%? Very probably it would be the second, but the salesman has done twice as much damage.

Pricing is very, very important, but it's often given much less consideration than it deserves. Much less consideration, in fact, than areas such as sales volume and fixed cost which, as we have seen above, have lower impact. And yet, I have seen more badly thought out, perverse or plain suicidal behaviour in this area than in just about any other.

Case Study – Pricing in an Information Business

To see value based pricing in its purest form, look at an information business. When one piece of information, or one piece of programming work, can be delivered to tens of thousands of additional people at no extra cost, cost becomes irrelevant. Value is the only way of setting price.

For example, a company maintained and sold access to a very large database of scientific and technical information. They were approached by one of their largest customers, a global pharmaceutical company. This customer wanted a customised interface. The company estimated that giving the customer what they wanted would take 12 programmer days.

The fee quoted (and accepted): one million pounds.

This shows what you can do in a pure information business. Your business probably isn't online information, but many businesses are information, or knowledge, businesses even if they don't look that way at first. Even if they are not, there is often scope for better pricing strategies.

Here is a list of clues that you have scope for clever pricing:

You sell to a range of different customers, who have different ideas about value and different levels of willingness to pay. The fact is that value is in the eye of the purchaser, and you have no idea what it is. I used to have a speech on pricing which I gave to chief executive groups, and to illustrate the point I started by asking them what they would pay for my fountain pen. The actual shop price was £15, but I had responses ranging from 25p to £150. Some of the extreme figures were probably not entirely serious, but there was still a genuinely wide range. This made sense, as I pointed out, when you thought about what was in the mind of potential purchaser. If I just wanted a reasonably stylish, interesting-looking pen then I would probably have been willing to pay £15 or £20. If I wanted something for my son to use at school I would have wanted to pay less than that. On the other hand, maybe my wife used to have a similar pen (which by the way was part of a set) and had lost it, I would have been happy to pay £30, maybe even £50, to replace it for her.

You have a high gross margin. That is, you can make or supply additional units at relatively low cost. This is true of information products – books, CDs, software – but is also true of many other types of product and service. For example, Starbucks offers a loyalty card scheme with a very generous incentive to join – a large cup of filter coffee for only £1, which is about half the cost of any similar sized drink in the shop. They can do this because the gross profit on the cup of coffee is very high – the ingredients are water and a small amount of coffee, giving a margin in excess of 90%. Most of Starbucks' costs are fixed – rent, salaries – giving it scope to do clever things with pricing. In the case of the loyalty card scheme, their calculation is that they can still make some money on each cup and if they offer a strong incentive the extra number of cups they sell will more than compensate for the lower price. Notice how the offer also addresses, and splits off, a particular customer group. They are the ones who are predisposed to visit regularly (otherwise it's not worth the effort of getting the card) and sufficiently price-sensitive to choose the cheaper filter coffee.

The business is a knowledge business, that is to say that the value of the product, and much of its cost, comes from the knowledge used in research and development and design, not the cost of manufacture. This is not essential – it would after all be hard to characterise Starbucks as a knowledge business – but it is a strong indicator that there is scope for intelligent pricing. In fact, it is probably an indicator that intelligent pricing is essential. In such a business pricing based on cost of production risks underselling the product, failing to recover the cost of the research that went into developing it, and failing to fund the research needed to develop the products of the future.

The product or service is distinctive. This is helpful, but by no means essential. Starbucks, for example, is just one of many chains of coffee shops, offering similar things. Despite that, it manages to use a number of sophisticated pricing strategies.

These criteria give you a clue as to how to set prices intelligently. The approach can be summed up like this:

- Understand your customers, and the value they place on your offering. Recognise that different types of customers have very different ideas about value.

- As far as possible, deal with customers as individuals, and offer them prices based on their own perceptions of value.

- As far as possible, offer a distinctive product, or present your offering in a distinctive way. The more you can do this, the better your chances of being paid close to the full value of what you offer.

> ### Case Study – Engineering is a Knowledge Business
>
> In a European engineering group, both the UK and the Italian businesses were sometimes asked to help solve engineering problems – customers didn't just want to buy components, they needed help in designing systems that would give deliver a particular performance, or fit into a particularly awkward space.
>
> In the UK, these projects were priced according to a well-established and widely understood pricing model of cost of components plus around 30%, giving a margin of approximately 25%.
>
> The Italians, on the other hand, didn't have a pricing

model. They had a pricing process based on "let's all get in a huddle and think of a number". Very Italian, but also very effective. It produced margins of up to 70% where their British colleagues would have settled for 25%. The point which the Italians understood and the British didn't was this: sometimes they were not selling components, but solutions to difficult engineering problems. The customers couldn't solve these problems, but would gladly pay for someone else to do so.

The interesting thing about this engineering company was that it was not in any way high-tech. The product range had remained unchanged for a couple of decades. The real value was not in the components, but in the expertise relating to their use. This wasn't relevant in every case – often the customer just needed a replacement part for an old machine – but when it was, it was hugely valuable.

Case Study – Vaccines in the Developing World

In June 2011 the global pharmaceutical company GSK announced that it would sell its rotavirus gastroenteritis vaccine available in the developing world at a price only 5% of that charged in the developed world. This was clearly a wonderful thing for people in the developing world, and excellent PR for GSK. It was not, however, pure altruism – it made good commercial sense. GSK would sell almost no vaccines in the developing world if they kept to the developed world price, but they still cover their manufacturing costs if they sold at the lower price. The sales in the developed world would recover the cost of developing the vaccine and funding future research, while developing world sales made a small but worthwhile additional contribution.

See how this example illustrates many of the criteria for differentiated pricing:

- There is a high gross margin. Once the vaccine has been developed and licensed, GSK can make additional doses at a relatively very low cost.

- There are two markets, developed world and developing world, which have very different levels of willingness and ability to pay.

- The product is distinctive – in fact protected by patents.

The challenge for GSK is to ensure that the lower-priced products do not leak back into the higher-priced markets. If it can do this, then this two-tier pricing strategy benefits everybody.

Segmenting the Market – Individually

In an ideal world, all prices would be set this way. In practice, of course, you need to have a product with some distinctiveness (otherwise you will never get too far away from competitive prices) and the sale needs to be large enough to make it worthwhile engaging with the customer to explore their value preferences and how you can best meet them. Here are the things to do when those conditions apply.

Consider how important your offering is to them. One of my clients sold banking software, which banks used to automate and improve the functioning of their back offices. Different banks could see the value of the software in very different ways. Some were looking to improve the efficiency of their back office and so reduce costs. In this case, there was a relatively straightforward financial case to be made – we spend so much on software, we save so many heads in the back office. Other customers, however, were in a very different frame of mind. They were desperately struggling to meet regulatory reporting requirements, and if they failed they would have been shut down. In this case there was no return on investment calculation – it was a question of survival.

I have often been surprised by how blind technology vendors, in particular, can be to the priorities of their clients and prospects. I remember one case in which, newly appointed as CFO of a software company, I found that one of the revenue streams, accounting for about one third of the total, was basically out of control. It went up and down each month. People were convinced that the numbers were wrong, that we probably weren't billing everything we should have done, but nobody could explain what was going on because the reporting was so poor. I was practically jumping up and down with frustration, and asked the vendors of the accounting system in to see if they could give me something that would solve my problem. They did indeed have a reporting tool that would do the job, but they completely failed to recognise my frustration and sense of urgency. In the end they came up with a small proposal containing a confusing range of options with a very small price tag. If instead they had just said "we will come in, install the software and build the reports you need," I would have said yes on the spot and happily paid 10 times the fee they quoted.

Try to make your offering look as distinctive as possible by offering a solution, not a product.

Creating Customer Groups

Most businesses will not be able to deal with their customers individually, as the size of the sale just does not justify the exploration needed. In that case, the best approach is to identify different subgroups in the market and offer something tailored to them.

Here is a long list of ways of doing this:

Delay

In many, many fields different customers are more or less in a hurry, and represent different markets that will pay different prices. When it comes to online stock prices, for example, active traders need information which is totally up to date and pay handsomely for it. Those who, on the other hand, just want to track their portfolios from time to time can get very nearly the same data for free from many websites, which license it at low rates from the same information providers who charge the active traders such large amounts. The difference is that the information on the website is always delayed by at least 15 minutes, making it useless for the active traders but good enough for the more casual user.

There are other ways of using delay to distinguish between the customers who really, really want your offering and those who are a little lukewarm. Book publishers, for example, have been doing it for ages. A new book comes out first in hardback and then, after a time, in paperback at around half the price. The difference in price has very little to do with the extra cost of making the hardback – it has everything to do with charging the very impatient, the people who must have it as soon as possible, extra.

Convenience

This is hardly new, but remains a much underexploited technique. The convenience store understands very well that it is selling convenience, not products – prices there are higher than in a supermarket, but the store is closer to where you live and you don't have to queue at the checkout. Where else could this applied?

A few years ago, I gave a short talk on pricing to a group of business people. One of the audience, a mortgage broker, left the meeting and immediately implemented a two-tier pricing policy. For no fee, he would see you in his office during office hours. This appealed to the first time buyers who were counting every penny. For a fee, he would visit you at home or at your place of work, at your convenience. This appealed to the richer homeowners who weren't particularly concerned about a fee but valued their time. This two-tier scheme raised his average fee considerably, and didn't actually involve him in any extra work – he had previously been visiting people at their convenience for no extra.

There are more opportunities to offer more convenience in return for higher prices. I am still waiting for plumber or home repair service who promises to make you the first call of the day. That way, you know exactly when they will arrive, and you don't waste time waiting in for them. Surely that's worth something extra?

The Subtracted-Value Version

Many of these ideas are for added value offerings, faster, more convenient, more features or functions. There is also scope for the subtracted-value version. This is a way of making a sale to people who are not currently buying. The trick is to offer them something which is cheap enough to appeal to them, but does not appeal to your existing market.

A good example of this was the IBM laser printer series E. This was originally aimed at the office market, and printed 10 sheets per minute. IBM realised that the machine was too expensive for the small office/home office ("soho") market. They could have sold it there at a lower price, and made money. In the soho market they only needed to cover their manufacturing costs – the corporate market was paying for the design and development. The problem was that if they did start selling in the soho market at a lower price, the corporate buyers would soon realise and start buying there. Then there would be nobody to cover the development costs.

IBM solved the problem by producing a lower cost, lower-performance version of the printer, printing only five sheets per minute. This was too slow for the corporate market. The only difference between the two models was an extra line of software in the slower model, telling it "wait."

There is something rather counterintuitive about making an extra effort to produce an inferior product, but that is the logic of subtracted value. FedEx reportedly use this approach with deliveries. They offered a service with guaranteed delivery before 10am and another guaranteed before 12. If they happened to arrive before 10 am with a "before 10" and a "before 12" package, they would not deliver the second one but make a second call later in the morning.

Bundling

Bundling is a strategy for coping with, in fact profiting from, the fact that different customers value different things. Consider this example.

You sell software, specifically a word processor and a spreadsheet. To keep things simple, suppose that your customers are either marketing managers or accountants. The marketing managers mostly use the word processor, for which they would pay £200. The spreadsheet is of limited use to them, but they would pay £20 for it. The accountants' preferences are the exact opposite. The spreadsheet is very valuable, and they would pay £200. The word processor is worth £20.

If you had to sell the two products separately, your best strategy is to price both at £200. That way you sell the word processor to the marketing managers and the spreadsheet to the accountants, missing out on the smaller sales. If, on the other hand, you create a bundle of the two and call it an "office productivity package" then you can sell it for £220 both to accountants and marketing managers. You have raised revenue by 10% without any additional work, and your customers are enjoying more software.

Take some time to itemise the different products and services you offer, and look at who buys them. If you find that very few customers buy all or most of your range, bundling could be a way to raise sales, and also customer satisfaction.

When All Else Fails, There's Always The Goldilocks Principle
In this case, the temptation is to despair – to set a price based on "intuition" (which in this case means guesswork), or matching the competition, or cost-plus. This runs two risks, one very obvious and one less obvious but more deadly. The obvious risk is of getting the price wrong and either leaving money on the table by asking for too little, or losing profitable sales by asking for too much.

The second risk, however, is deadlier. It is the risk of never finding out what is possible and what is not. We may get it wrong the first time, in fact we very probably will, but we must give ourselves a way of realising and correcting our error. Guesswork, matching the competition or cost-plus won't give us that possibility, but there is a method that will. It's called the Goldilocks principle, named after the little girl in the fairy story who looked for the porridge that was "r too hot, not too cold, but just right."

Here is how the coffee shop applied the Goldilocks principle. In the beginning they just sold a cup of coffee, "standard" size. Then they added a large size, which appealed to some of their customers. Then came the stroke of genius. They introduced the extra large (in Starbucks that's a pint of coffee). Some people took the extra large, but the more significant effect was that lots of people who previously took standard moved up to large. The reason was that "large" wasn't large any more – it was medium. We all have strong tendency to "avoidance of extremes," so the middle option is always appealing to us.

Goldilocks lets us hedge our bets when it comes to pricing, and it also, crucially, allows us to learn. We know that there are very probably some high-value customers out there, but we can't work out who they are. Goldilocks lets them identify themselves by the choices they make. Then we can observe them, work out why they attach so much value to what we offer them and start to develop more precisely tailored offerings for them.

We can also work on refining our pricing scheme. If we notice that lots of people take the highest value option, that suggests that some of them would take something even ˈher-value if we offered it to them. We can raise the price ˈarge, or even add a whole new option above – , "large" becomes the new "standard", new "large".

Conversely, if we see that almost nobody takes highest-value option but many of them go for the lowest, that suggests that prices may have been set too high and we are losing customers at the bottom of the price range. We can adjust our pricing scheme to capture these lower-value customers (always provided that they are profitable, of course). Remove the most expensive option and add a new one cheaper than the previous cheapest.

Case Study – Suicidal Incentives

In a competitive market for magazine advertising, a hard-driving sales director had set his team aggressive targets for sales volume. They rose to the challenge. Unfortunately, the sales director hadn't said much about rates, as a result of which they ended up selling space for 20% of what their competitors were charging. That's not 20% less, but five pages for the price of one. This sort of thing is quickly done, but takes years to recover from.

Case Study – the Ultimate in Pricing Chutzpah

What do you do about the really low-price customer? The one who just wants to pay as little as possible? Here's what happened when I went to buy a new washing machine.

As far as I'm concerned, a washing machine is just a washing machine. I just want to pay as little as possible. I

John Lewis in Oxford Street – a Zanussi because the packaging was damaged. about that – only the packaging was damaged, the machine was perfect.

While I waited for delivery, I reflected. "I think it's a trick," I told my wife. "I think they go into the warehouse and deliberately damage the packaging. It's a way of giving big discounts to the really price-sensitive customers like me, and not to the others."

When the machine did turn up, surprise! Not just the machine, but the packaging was pristine.

How Cost Plus Pricing Will Destroy Your Business:

Cost-plus pricing has its attractions:

- It's easy to understand and administer

- It seems "fair"

- It requires no insight into customer psychology or expectations.

Its only drawback is that it can destroy you.

Case Study – Cost Plus Pricing

The engineering company was under pressure on profits, and was responding by developing sources in Eastern Europe and the Far East. This was saving them money, but...

They operated a cost plus pricing system. This meant that every €100 they saved on materials resulted in a reduction of selling price of around €130.

They were cost saving their way out of business.

Fast Action Plan on Pricing

Here are the principles for very profitable pricing:

Base your pricing on value to the customer, not cost of production. Remember how this worked for the database company. Cultivate an attitude of "we provide a quality product which deserves a premium price" throughout the organisation.

As far as possible, deal with customers as individuals, with their own ideas about value – as the engineering company did, understanding when it was solving tricky problems and when it was just supplying parts.

If you can't deal with customers as individuals, give them options, as Starbucks does.

Make sure that your sales staff know how to uncover customer value and negotiate prices accordingly. Design their incentives to encourage them to maintain pricing, not chase after volume (don't fall into the same trap as the magazine publishers).

Make sure that you have the information you need to track what everyone is doing on pricing.

Think carefully about moving control over pricing up a level or two in the organisation – from sales rep to sales manager, or sales manager to sales director, or sales director to CEO.

Abolish Cost-plus Pricing.

Now work through the process step by step:

Think whether you are more likely to find additional revenues above your present price point or below. It will depend on the business you are in. Consultancies or technology firms who solve difficult one-off problems are more likely to generate additional revenues by charging more for truly valuable work, while hotels and airlines are very good at making money from the bottom of the pyramid – the people who are happy to book at the last minute or travel off-peak but who, in the absence of a really cheap deal, wouldn't go at all.

Next, think about whether the value you provide is created when you provide the good or the service, or whether it comes from the work you have done prior to that moment. This is particularly important if you see potential in higher value offerings. If you are a consultant, or a manufacturer of hi-tech equipment, you may be able to solve in moments a problem which has perplexed your customer for years. You can do this because of the years you have spent learning to do what you do. That is the value that you deliver to the customer, and that is what you need to be paid for. It has nothing to do with how long it takes you to assess that particular situation and make a recommendation, or the cost of materials and assembly that go into your product.

Next, decide how much you can segment your market.

Can you deal with customers as individuals? This is the obvious choice for consultancies or designers or bespoke software solutions, but it can work well for simpler services as well. It could for instance be applied by personal trainers or garden maintenance companies. What is most important is that customers are sufficiently few in number and large in value for it to be worth the time taken to develop a personalised offering.

If you can't deal with customers as individuals, think about dividing them into different groups, each of which has a different idea about value. Airlines do this when they offer different fares to business and leisure travellers (keeping the business travellers away from the leisure fares by requiring a stay over a Saturday night).

If you can't see logical groups, apply the Starbucks

solution – offer three choices and let the customers segregate themselves.

Now you are ready to work out how to approach your market.

Organise your different customers, or customer groups, into a hierarchy, as in the diagram, and identify or create the offering that matches them. For each level, be clear about what it is about the offering that makes it worth them spending more instead of buying further down the pyramid, and what stops customers from higher up the pyramid migrating downwards.

Customer	Offering	Why they won't migrate downwards	Why customers from higher levels won't buy
High value – traders	Real time stock prices	They need real time information	Not applicable
Low value – website users	Quotes delayed by 15 minutes	Not applicable	Not real time

CHAPTER NINE

CUSTOMERS AND PRODUCTS

Be Prepared For A Shock

If you haven't looked at the profitability of individual products and customers, make sure you do. It's a guaranteed shocker. Finding out the truth about profitability by customer or by product is one of the most powerful ways of improving profitability.

Try the following six questions to see whether this is a fruitful area for you:

1. Can you, within 30 minutes, identify your Top 10 customers, by profit not revenue?

2. Can you, within 30 minutes, identify your bottom 10 customers, by profit not revenue?

3. Are you absolutely sure that these figures include all the funny little costs that tend to creep in, like special packaging, emergency freight, marketing support, customisation, unusual levels of returns or complaints, extended payment terms…

4. Can you, within 30 minutes, tell me the difference in profitability between old customers and new customers?

5. Can you give me the profitability of your different types of customer (e.g. large corporate/small corporate/SME, or OEM vs end user)?

6. Can you pick out the anomalies in customer groups? If one type of customer is usually very profitable, which few are not, and why?

Do the same for products. In my experience, fewer than 10% of companies can answer yes to all six, and yet this information is enormously valuable.

Case Study – Big Customers are not Good Customers

I was told this story when I was talking to a group of Chief Executives in Yorkshire.

"A friend of mine is head of a confectionery company. It's a major supplier of pick-n-mix, one of the things Woolworths was famous for. Woolworths had gone bust three months ago. For a long time I didn't dare ask him how things were going. They must have been dire, given how important Woolworths was to him. In the end, I plucked up courage and asked him, how's business?

"'Great', he replied. 'When Woolworths went down, we had 100 field sales people servicing them. I sent some of them off in this direction, some of them in that... we've picked up this, we're getting a pick-n-mix counter in Tesco... overall, sales are down 40% but profits are up by 25%.'"

When you do your customer profitability work, cast a sceptical eye over the really important customers. Yes, they take a lot of volume, but they take full advantage of the bargaining power that gives them. And then you have all the costs of the special requests and extended payment terms. It's not unusual, I find, that a client's largest customer is costing them money, or is at best marginally profitable.

Even when there is no obvious big customer, there can be huge value in understanding the profitability of different customers.

Case Study – Small Customers can be Problematic too

An engineering company in Spain had 700 customers which it served by means of visits from field sales reps. I was there because it was struggling to make money. An 80/20 analysis showed the usual, unsurprising result – 141 of those customers accounted for 80% of gross profit.

There was however a twist. The cost of a visit by a rep was €150. At that rate, 200 of the customers were not placing enough business to cover the cost of the rep's visit, never mind contribute to any of the company's other costs.

The action was clear. We couldn't have reps visiting these customers. That didn't mean abandoning them, but finding a more cost-effective way of serving them – by telephone, email or mail.

Customers, Products or Something Else?

Does it make sense to look at products first, or at customers? The answer is that it depends on a number of factors, and in some cases the right answer might be "neither". Here is how to approach it.

Firstly, sometimes it is clear that your business is a product/service-focused business, or a customer-focused business. The product-focused business puts all its energy and ingenuity into producing a product or service, and then tries to sell it to as many customers as possible. A customer-focused business, on the other hand, has a group of customers and tries to offer them as wide a range of services as it can.

Sometimes it's very clear which is the dominant factor. If you are a pig farmer, then you are in a product business. You sell pigs. Your customers may be supermarkets, who also buy beef, mutton, milk, cornflakes, children's clothes and all the many, many things that supermarkets sell, but you don't for a moment consider offering any of those. Pig farming is what you know, pigs are what you sell.

A bank, on the other hand, is a good example of a customer-focused business. It's hard for banks to get new customers (it has been claimed that most bank customers are more likely to get divorced and change their spouse than they are to change their bank), so they concentrate on selling more and more products to the customers they already have. The list is long – current accounts, savings accounts, unit trusts, insurance, mortgages....

Sometimes, though, it isn't clear which is the dominant factor. For example, you might be in the plumbing business. You could be service-driven, meaning that you only do plumbing. Maybe you only do emergency plumbing. In this case you don't get that much repeat business, but instead work hard to make sure that yours is the first name that springs to mind when something springs a leak, and that you always answer the phone when someone calls (the biggest failure of emergency maintenance services, in my experience). On the other hand, you could give your plumbing business a customer focus. You could work to develop relationships with customers who had substantial, regular requirements for plumbing services – local authorities with housing stock, large private landlords or housing associations, contractors who build or refurbish houses or flats.

The other way to work out whether you are product/service or customer-focused business is to stop thinking about it and just look at the numbers. That is how the Spanish engineering company mentioned in the case study above did it. I had no preconceptions, but simply wanted to find a way of cutting the data in a way that made different parts of the business look different. First I looked at different products, but this wasn't very helpful. Everything had fairly similar margins, so there wasn't any very obvious scope for doing more of some and less of something else.

Looking at the data by customer, on the other hand, was very revealing. This was because there was a high cost associated with serving a customer, most of which was independent of how much they bought. Once we put the cost of visiting the customer against the gross profit generated, we could see that some customers were highly profitable and others were losing money. There was also some interesting information to be gained from looking at the cost of order processing. One customer in particular placed hundreds of very small orders. The average gross profit per order was €9, but the cost of processing that order was €10. This customer didn't even generate enough profit to cover the administrative cost of processing the order.

The conclusion in this case was that this company could do well on all its product lines, provided it was selling to the right sort of customer in the right way. To be worth a visit from a field sales rep a customer had to place a minimum amount of business, although it didn't matter too much what exactly they bought. For the smaller customers, the challenge was to find a way of making sales that didn't involve expensive rep visits and so could be profitable.

Understanding whether you are fundamentally a product/service-focused company or a customer-focused company is vital to taking sensible decisions. If you are a product/service-focused company and a particular product or service is not profitable, then it is perfectly acceptable to drop it.

If on the other hand you are a customer-focused company then the same decision would be suicidal. Consider a bank, for example. The basic current account is unprofitable, but that isn't a reason for ceasing to offer it. The current account is essential to the customer relationship which allows the bank to offer all the other, more profitable, services. Don't drop the current account unless you want to say goodbye to all that other business as well! If you can find a way of identifying and segregating customers who only want a current account and will never, ever ask for anything else then it could make sense to look at your marketing and make sure it doesn't attract too many of them, but be careful. It's probably better to spend your time looking for ways to sell extra products to the customers who are interested in them.

By the same token, if you are the plumbing business which works with large landlords, don't jump to conclusions if you find some particular type of work which loses money. If the overall customer profitability is acceptable, and this particular unappealing type or work is important to the customer, then live with it.

Sometimes the correct focus is neither customers nor products, but productive capacity. If your business is based on large fixed assets which cost much the same whether they are used or not, then you need to look at matters differently. Examples for this type of business include printing companies, shipping lines, airlines, and owners of large online databases. In all these businesses a large bulk of the cost is incurred in acquiring or building the asset – the printing press, the ship, the aircraft or the database – and the cost of one extra supply – one extra copy printed, container or passenger transported or database record accessed – is relatively small.

In this case it becomes quite arbitrary to allocate cost to a particular job or customer, since so much of it is incurred anyway. In this case the proper unit for analysis is the asset. Does it, overall, recover its costs? Does every customer, every product produced, at least cover the additional, marginal cost, of supplying it?

The tricky thing here is to deal with the marginal cost problem. Consider the printing firm. Here it can make perfect sense to take on a job which just covers the cost of ink and paper (we will assume that no overtime is worked, so if we didn't take the job we would still have to pay our workers to come to work and stand around). We receive a net benefit, a contribution towards fixed cost, but there is a problem. We can't take on all work on this basis, because something needs to pay for the cost of the press and the workforce. How do we decide which products or customers are acceptable if they just cover marginal cost, and which have to make an acceptable contribution to all the other costs?

The answer is in two of the other chapters here. Firstly, we need a pricing scheme that looks at value. And secondly, we need to minimise unused capacity. When we price a job, we must ignore the fact that we could do it for very little marginal cost. We must make sure that we charge close to the full value of the job, and that we have enough jobs for which the value is large enough to cover the full cost of the operation. Then, and only then, can we start looking for work at lower prices which makes no more than a "contribution to overhead".

Fast Action Plan on Customers and Products

It's a three stage process:

1. Identify all costs arising from making the product, providing the service and serving the customer and allocate them to those products, services and customers.

2. Look for patterns. Which customer and product groups are particularly profitable, or not? Why?

3. Take action. Mobilise people to look for more of the best types of products or customers. Deal with the worst – fix them, or drop them.

Warning – Don't Go Overboard

This is an area where it is dangerously easy to become stuck in a swamp. "Paralysis by analysis" is a real risk. Here are some ways to avoid the pitfalls and produce some worthwhile results. Here are the ways of reducing the risk:

Go for quick results. Don't make this into a big project. Think of it as a small project, followed by another small project, followed by another. Each project produces a return, which generates the momentum and motivation for the next one. Start, for example, by looking for the single most profitable customer, or customer type. Once you have identified that, get everyone working on finding more of the same type and then look for the next most profitable type. Or make your next project a hunt for the least profitable group.

Use the 80/20 rule as discussed in Chapter One. 20% of customers make 80% of the profit. A different 20% produce 80% of the drag on profits. Once you have identified these two groups, you have obtained 80% of the value of the exercise with 20% of the total effort. Maybe now it's time to stop.

Be hypothesis-driven, as explained in Chapter Four. Make shrewd guesses and then test them. It will get you to useable results much more quickly.

Look for shortcuts. Once I had to do a product profitability analysis in a specialist printing firm with about 10 different printing processes. I was going to have to work out the unit costs printing on 10 different production lines, something that had never been considered before. It was going to be a big job. Then I discovered that the company had recently considered outsourcing a large part of its production, and had obtained quotes from external suppliers for exactly those costs I needed to calculate, covering about 60% or the product range. I could assume that my client's costs were at least equal to these. A week's work collapsed into a couple or hours.

A way to identify unprofitable clients: ask everyone: "it's 4.30 on a Friday. The phone rings – it's a customer. Who do you least want it to be?" If several people give you the same names, you have a prime suspect.

Identifying all the Costs

This again is a three step process:

1. Identify all those costs which are aren't captured by product or customer, but need to be

2. Calculate the cost

3. Allocate that cost to products and customers.

Look at all the activities involved in serving a client or making a product. These will probably include, but not be limited to:

- Selling (in person, by phone or by mail)

- Presales activity – advising them on the right version to order, answering questions

- Order processing – if it's a physical product, picking, packing and despatching

- After–sales service, dealing with problems and queries

- Invoicing

- Cash collection

There are two ways to calculate the unit cost of an activity. Where it is clear how much time is being spent on it, take the total cost of that time and divide by the number of units. For instance, we know that a field sales rep spends all his or her time visiting customers, or doing things which support that activity. So if it costs say £5,000 per month to run a field sales person (salary, social security, travel etc) and they visit 40 customers a month, then the cost per sales visit is £125.

Sometimes the situation is more complicated. Suppose for example that order processing is handled by several people, all of whom also do other things. One way to do it would be analogous to what we did for the salesman work out the cost of the time spent on order processing based on the cost of employing the people and the percentage of their time that they spend on it. However, it may be difficult to get at that percentage if they are constantly switching between activities.

An alternative is to work out the hourly cost of employing the person, observe the average amount of time taken for an activity and use that to calculate the unit cost. For example, if it costs £20 per hour on average to employ the people who process orders and the average order takes 15 minutes to process, then the cost of an order is £5.

Here is an example of how to calculate the cost of order processing.

An Example Company

Order Fulfilment Unit Costs

£, based on salary and social security costs, excluding any other overhead allocation

	Full Cost	% Allocated to Order Fulfilment	Cost Allocated to Order Fulfilment
Employees - Salary and social security			
Order Processing Staff			
Case	26,389	100%	26,389
Gamble	27,489	100%	27,489
Housman	20,617	100%	20,617
Vachs	48,433	15%	7,265
Martin	26,664	0%	0
Francis	44,507	80%	35,606
Warehouse Staff			
Johnson	28,824	100%	28,824
3 others	60,235	65%	39,153
Total Order Fulfilment Cost			185,343
Number of Order Lines			17,000
Total Cost per Order Line			10.9

Once you have the unit costs, you need to allocate them to customers and products. This is in two stages.

Firstly, allocate the costs of the operations equally, using the most sensible basis.

So for example the cost of order processing is allocated by order line. The cost of account management is allocated per customer. Mostly it will be quite clear which is the most appropriate basis to use, but sometimes it might be open to debate. Does customer service depend on customer (some customers are clueless, or trying to do very complex things with your product), or product (some products are just inherently easy to use).

Secondly, look for any customers or products who make disproportionately large or small demands, and allocate accordingly. For instance:

Customer A places orders via the website, and rarely needs to talk to anyone or causes any complications. Their cost of order processing per order is therefore reduced to 50% of the standard.

Customer B generates huge amount of work in credit control. They constantly query invoices, send money which is hard to relate to invoices outstanding, and need constant chasing. Their share of credit control costs is three times the standard.

Product C generates large amounts of customer service activity – customers just seem to find it difficult to use. You have verified that this is because of the product, not the customer, and this product gets twice the standard allocation of customer service costs.

Use discretion when it comes to the second stage. This is where the risk of paralysis by analysis is at its highest. Don't make special adjustments unless you have some good reason to suppose that there is a significant difference, and that the effect of that difference would be significant. Usually, the results of the first stage are so gross that in most cases there is no need to refine. The most profitable customers would still be the most profitable even if they had to pick up twice their share of account management costs. The least profitable products would still be the least profitable even if the picked up half the standard cost for customer service.

Pitfalls

The biggest risk here is losing sight of the objective. The objective is not to produce a complete and accurate analysis of costs across all customers and all products. It is not even to identify the largest opportunities for improvement (although that would be good, and usually you will achieve this). The objective is to obtain some actionable insights which repay the cost of doing the work. Beyond the risk of paralysis by analysis, there are two other main risks to getting a benefit from this process.

The first is lack of buy-in. The results of this exercise can be quite shocking. They may surprise many people. Sacred cows may need to be slaughtered. Some people may end up looking rather bad. To deal with this, one essential is that everyone believes the data. There are two ways to ensure this. The first is to keep the analysis simple. The second is to ensure that any assumptions (like how time is spent, whether Customer X consumes two times or four times its fair share of customer service time) are validated with the people who manage the relevant areas. If everyone can see a clear simple link between what they said went on in their area and what the final results show, then they are much more likely to believe and take action on the results. If you obscure that link with an overcomplicated analysis or, even worse, by making assumptions yourself about what other people do, you have lost and will spend the rest of your life debating whether the results are accurate, rather than what to do with them.

The second risk is being too simplistic. The numbers need to be put in context. For instance:

- Product A is not very profitable, but it is essential to retain a group of customers who are, in total, highly profitable.

- Product B is not profitable, but it is new and has high potential once it starts selling in quantity

- Customer C does not look very attractive at present, but if we can persuade them to start taking the new product range they would look very different.

These could all be valid points, but they could also be excuses for inertia. They needed to be treated with respect but also with a level of healthy scepticism. How essential is product A in retaining that attractive group of customers? Who says so? If it is important to those customers, is there a way of obtaining a price rise?

How long has the "new" product B been on sale? Are there signs of it taking off? If not, how much longer do we want to wait?

Similarly, how long have we been working on customer C to take the new product line? What progress are we making? How much longer do we want to give it? In dealing with these questions, remember that it's not between continuing to support product A, product B or product C. It is a choice between allocating effort to those areas or redirecting it to other, potentially more fruitful ones.

Put another way, there is always an opportunity cost to what we do. It's not whether there is some benefit to what we're doing, but whether there is more benefit doing something else. This gives you some leverage for change. Every time someone advocates putting effort into maintaining the status quo, ask what the alternative would be. If we stopped doing that, what could we do instead? If we redirect our efforts towards finding more of the really profitable customers and products (now that we know so much more about which they are), what could we achieve?

Action

The end result will look something like this:

Customer	Sales	Reported gross profit	Order processing costs	Special packaging costs	Sales visits	Actual profit
A	10,000	5,000	200	300	2,000	2,500
B	10,000	5,000	500	0	500	4,000

Reported gross profit is what comes out of the accounting system: sales less cost of goods sold.

The analysis shows that although the two customers at first appear to have the same profitability, they are in fact very different. A places relatively few small orders which gives it a low cost of order processing, but has special packaging requirements and requires a lot of sales attention.

B on the other hand places more, smaller orders but is much more straightforward to serve, making it substantially more profitable. You may do the analysis for all customers, for just a few, or for representative types. Once you have it, you can work out where to put your effort.

Now, make sure it happens:

- Strategy/Objectives: Are you clear about the profile of the ideal client and the best product? Has this been communicated to everyone? Does your strategy recognise that some products and customers are much more profitable than others?

- Organisation: Who is responsible for tracking customer and product profitability at a detailed level? It involves many different functions, so who coordinates or drives it?

- Information and incentives: How good is your information? Do your incentives encourage sales people to sell the most profitable products to the most profitable customers rather than focus on what's easiest or most familiar?

- Skills: You know which are the best products and best customers. Does the sales force have the product knowledge and selling skills best attuned to these?

CHAPTER TEN

SPARE CAPACITY

And Why It's Harder To Find Than You Think

In some businesses it is easy to spot whether you have excess capacity. If you are a professional service firm you will have everybody filling in time sheets and so will know whether you have enough work to keep everybody busy. If you are a taxi driver you will know if you are spending too much time waiting on a taxi rank or cruising around looking for a fare, rather than driving with a passenger in the back and the meter running. In many other areas, though, excess capacity can be harder to spot, and the opportunity therefore greater.

Spare capacity doesn't always manifest itself in people or machines lying idle. There are two features of organisations that tend to obscure its existence.

The first is the almost universal injunction to "keep busy". There are very few organisations where reading novels or comics at work, or leaving at 3pm because there is nothing else needing to be done that day, is considered acceptable behaviour. Quite the contrary – a well-managed organisation is considered to be one in which everyone is busy all the time. For many managers, "achieving optimum productivity" begins, and often ends, with making sure that everyone is occupied all the time. This would make sense only if we added one word to the injunction. There is no value in keeping everyone busy, only in keeping everyone *productively* busy. Forgetting that one word makes all the difference.

The problem is compounded by the fact that, if people are caught not being busy, it's usually considered to be their fault. When you look at it, this usually makes no sense. In an organisation of any complexity, the individual sits in the middle of a flow of work. If the person doing the step before hasn't finished their bit, I can't start on mine. If I work in production, I can't start before I receive the orders from sales. If I am a management accountant, I can't begin finalising the month until someone else has issued and entered all the sales invoices. This creates a problem if I can't do anything useful, for reasons outside my control.

If my lack of activity were seen as evidence of a system failure, or a delay elsewhere in the organisation, it would be useful sign that something might need attention. I would have no worries about letting it show, or even bringing it to someone's attention. Instead, I am more likely to be worried about being stigmatised for not being busy. Naturally enough, I cover it up. And, as anyone who has observed organisations for any length of time knows, there is no limit to human creativity when it comes to ways of looking busy when you are not. I remember in my first days as an auditor being intrigued, and rather puzzled, by an accounts clerk who spent hours reading the telephone directory, without ever turning the page. After a few days I understood – she spent most of her day chatting to her colleague at the opposite desk, and the phone book was there just as something to make her look occupied in case the big boss walked in. She was clearly under-employed, but she wasn't falling down on her work – the department was getting through its work and meeting its deadlines. At more senior levels, of course, the possibilities for generating time-consuming but unproductive work are even greater,

This example comes from the early 1980s, long before the internet was ever heard of, and makes me sceptical of all the news stories we hear about the shocking costs of employees doing Facebook, Twitter and personal email at work.

My own memories of 25 years of working life, based on observations of at least 100 workplaces (as auditor and consultant I got around a lot) convince me of two things. Firstly, that workplace timewasting is no worse now than it was in the technological Stone Age, even if its forms have changed. Secondly, that very few people waste time at work when there is useful work to be done. If timewasting is going on, it is the organisation, not the individual that is wasting the time by not organising matters so that the individuals have productive things to do.

The second feature of organisations which makes spare capacity hard to spot is the well-known Parkinson's Law: work expands to fill the space available. (I would add: "and then expands some more").This is even harder to deal with. In the case of looking busy the individual at least knows what they are doing, and why. In the case of Parkinson's Law, nobody knows what is happening. Early in my career I had a dramatic illustration of this.

I worked for an American oil company in London. The finance department consisted of 20 people in London and another 50 in Aberdeen, the main operational base. Following a change of regime in Bakersfield, California, it was decided that the London office be closed. All finance tasks would be moved to Aberdeen. The 20 finance staff were redundant, but offered the chance to relocate. Only one accepted.

I was genuinely concerned about how the people in Aberdeen would cope with all the extra work, given that there were no plans to recruit extra staff there. With the state of the job market there at that time, extra people would have been hard to find in any case. I needn't have worried. I was friends with some of the people in Aberdeen, and gave one of them a call six months later. How had they managed with all the extra work? No problem, he told me. They just took it on, with no extra people needed. This was quite stunning. We had lost 19 people. Even if you assume that we saved two by not needing anyone to account specifically for the London office, we were 17 bodies down. That is a loss of 85% of the London staff, or 24% – one quarter – of total UK staff, apparently without any impact on operations. And yet everyone in London genuinely believed that they were doing useful, necessary work and doing it efficiently.

At this point, the more gung-ho managers may be forming a thought like this: "Excellent. So I could just arbitrarily cut out 25% of capacity, and we could still get the work done". Beware. It is not that simple. It would be good to think that squeezing numbers, piling on the pressure, would result in effort being redirected to what matters most, but that wouldn't necessarily happen, as the next example shows.

A marketing consultancy had been successful, won several large new accounts, and had the chance to pitch for several more. Unfortunately, the strain was beginning to tell. Everyone was overloaded, and the average working week was heading towards 50 hours. For the first time, they took a serious look at the information from their timesheet system. What this showed was alarming. Although time was desperately short and every day was a battle to juggle priorities and get work out on time, only 55% of the hours being worked were spent on anything useful, namely working on projects and pitches. The rest was going into the category "administration" – interminable meetings, reports, updates... nothing that produced a result. It seemed bizarre, but it illustrates a principle time in many organisations isn't allocated according to the importance of the task, but according to the importance of the person making the request. When making the request they may not stop to think, or even know, what actually produces results. In this case, with a detailed attention to utilisation rates the consultancy was able to raise the percentage of time spent on useful work from 55% to 70% within a couple of months.

It can be quite hard to assess how close to full capacity everything is, but there are reasonableness checks to be done. Work out the activity rate, and compare it with other benchmarks if you can find them. Even if you can't find external comparators, it can be revealing just to see what's going on. Here are some data from a study of an engineering company in Spain, with comments:

1. Salesmen handle 40 key accounts each – *surely* they can manage more than that?

2. Customer service staff process 25 order lines each per day – probably not bad, given that they often need to advise on the exact component needed and 20% of the time also have to order the part needed from another supplier.

3. Three warehouse staff pick and pack 75 order lines (25 shipments) per day – quite good, bearing in mind that they also assemble parts and do maintenance work, while maintaining a very fast service.

The comments are totally unscientific, based on nothing but intuition. Nevertheless, they do offer a way forward. There's no point in benchmarking points 1 and 3, as 1 is obviously too low and 3 is almost certainly OK. I can concentrate on examining point 2, and trying to find some external comparators.

The bottom line on excess capacity: it can exist in substantial way, and offer a worthwhile cost reduction opportunity. The harder it is to quantify utilisation, the less reporting you have on it, the bigger the opportunity. Don't expect anyone to tell you about the existence of excess capacity. When looking for it, be "hypothesis-driven." This is consultant-speak for having a suspicious mind, developing hypotheses by intuition and being creative in finding the information to confirm or deny them. Even if it's staring them in the face they may not have noticed it. Even if they have, they won't own up to it.

Fast Action Plan on Surplus Capacity

First, remind yourself of Parkinson's Law: work expands to fill the space available. This is not a joke – it's a documented fact of organisational life, and can be a significant drag on profitability.

Imagine a situation in which you have, say, an order processing department which could handle 200 orders per day but which only receives 100.

Three things could happen:

1. The staff organise amongst themselves to come in on alternate days

2. Everyone works hard all morning and then goes home for the day

3.   People find a way to look busy all day.

You know the answer could only be 3. People in organisations are very good at looking busy – I remember the clerk I met during my early career as an auditor who, whenever she wanted to stop work for a chat, would open the phone book in front of her.

Now you are in the right frame of mind.

When it comes to identifying spare capacity in practice, there are some standard techniques but you will also need to use your ingenuity to deal with specific cases.

Some standard techniques

The first standard technique is simply to look more closely. It may be a question of collecting data, or simply a question of paying more attention to it. If you are running machines, there are very cheap devices which you can attach to them to track whether they are running or not. Often I find timesheet systems used for billing, but not for tracking how time is being used. In that case the solution is very simple.

The second standard technique is to compare actual with theoretical. Let's say a department has 300 hours per week available to process transactions and the average transaction takes 15 minutes to process (you have observed, or have a good estimate). It should therefore be able to process 1,200 transactions in a week. What does it actually do? You may be surprised.

These two techniques will probably answer all your questions, but there may be some shortcuts available. This is where you will need to use some ingenuity. You may be able to benchmark between different locations which do the same job. Maybe you can make deductions from the amount of raw materials used. I have done this successfully with printing presses, counting the number of sheets of paper used in the month and comparing that with the number of sheets which could have been printed. It was a pretty approximate exercise, but since the conclusion was that the presses were running at between one third and one half of capacity, the lack of precision didn't matter.

CHAPTER ELEVEN

INCREASING EFFICIENCY

And Why You May Already Be Highly Efficient

Now we have arrived at where many efforts begin, but we are in good shape:

- We are generating much more cash

- We know what makes money and what doesn't

- We have some genuinely useful measures

You may find that you are much more efficient than you thought. On the other hand, it may turn out that "inefficiency" is profitable. It may be well worth spending the extra on short production runs or customised product if the customer is willing pay for it. As we start to deal with efficiency, we arrive at the point where it is possible to do serious damage. The measures we have looked at until now have been risk-free – introducing smarter pricing models or ditching unprofitable customers can only help, but reducing costs to boost efficiency can do damage.

Do You Want to Increase Efficiency?

This may seem an odd question, but it needs serious consideration. To explain why it matters, consider the workshop and the factory. The difference between the two is not a question of scale, but a question of mindset. The factory values efficiency, consistency and predictability. The workshop values flexibility and ingenuity. You could walk into a blacksmith's shop with a drawing of anything made of metal, and they could make it for you. You couldn't walk into a BMW car factory and ask them to make a Ford. A really clever blacksmith might spend some time with you, find out what you wanted your metal thing for, and suggest a better design. A factory will give you exactly what it has been designed to produce.

If you are a factory producing, say, baked beans for supermarkets to sell under their own label, then you compete on your ability to produce a product to a defined standard to a price. There are plenty of people who can meet the standard, so your success will come down to your ability to offer the lowest price.

What if, on the other hand, you are a consultancy which specialises in solving hard problems, or an advertising agency who wins business through its ability to out-think its competitors in coming up with creative solutions? In this case it is much less clear that efficiency matters. Clients choose you based on criteria such as flexibility, responsiveness, and "creativity" (the ability to do things that have never been done before). Your process is inherently messy and increasing efficiency is likely to make it harder to do what you do.

These examples are the two ends of the continuum. Your business is probably somewhere in the middle, but you need to be clear on where it sits in order to make a sensible decision about the correct trade off between efficiency and cost-effectiveness on the one hand and flexibility, responsiveness and creativity on the other.

Beware the Cost Boomerang

In May 2011 the accounting firm KPMG reported on a survey they had conducted of finance directors of UK companies. What proportion of the cost savings you have recently made, they asked, do you expect to reverse as the business starts to grow again? The answer was around 95%. Now some of this will be the natural result of rising levels of activity requiring additional costs, but much of it will be cost cutting being done in an unsustainable way. Consider some of the things these companies had done:

Cutting Training

This is one of the most popular ways to reduce spending in a hurry. But there are two problems. The first is that, sooner or later, you will feel the effect, in terms of lower productivity and lower morale. After some time, good people will start leaving. As well as this, think how your training requirement relates to other things you may be doing. Suppose that one of your other plans is to reduce the number of middle managers or supervisors, expecting each one to manage or supervise more people. This could be a good long term plan, but won't it make increased demands on the middle managers or supervisors who remain? They will benefit from help in meeting the new demands placed on them.

The Recruitment Freeze

This is a horrible idea. In effect, you are saying, "We are going to reduce staff numbers at random. It won't be quite random, though, as we will tweak the process slightly so that the better staff are more likely to leave."

This, after all, is the effect of the recruitment freeze. The effect is random, as it depends on who decides to leave. You may recognise that you need to increase your sales effort but can afford a reduction in marketing, but if a star salesperson leaves and a mediocre marketing person decides to stay, then by default you cut sales and maintain marketing. What makes it worse is that it will tend to be the better people who leave – they are the ones who have the better options elsewhere. The recruitment freeze feels less painful than taking hard decisions, but all you are doing is reshaping the organisation in a way that is basically random but will tend to reduce the average quality of your staff.

Holding Down Salaries

This works for a while, but sooner or later you will need to come to terms with the market. People aren't going to stay around forever if they see that they could be earning more elsewhere. The risk with the salaries freeze is that you suddenly, unexpectedly, reach a point where you need to raise salaries substantially, for a lot of people, or risk an exodus.

Cutting investment in the Future

This is so easy to do. It is made worse by accounting conventions, which don't properly distinguish between current spending, that which supports today's business, and investment, that which creates tomorrow's. Accountants have this demented idea that investment can only, as a rule, be a physical thing. If I buy a new computer, that's an investment. If I spend time, or commission a consultant to spend time, developing a plan to enter a new, rapidly growing market, or spend money on developing a new product or improving the product I already have, that cannot be shown as an investment. This problem with accountancy just adds to the other problem, which is that cutting spending on creating the future feels much less painful than cutting spending on today's business, because we don't feel the effect immediately. In fact, given the inherent imprecision of our view of the future, it is fatally easy to convince ourselves that there won't be an effect.

All these are temporary expedients. Some, like the salaries freeze, create the risk of damage in the future. Some, like cutting investment in new products or markets, create the certainty of damage in the future. You may have to apply them in case of necessity, but you need to be clear about what you are doing and what the risks are. You also need a way of balancing present and future to help you choose between different actions. This is the ROI rule.

Don't Forget About Risk

When reducing costs, we have fatal tendency to assume that we are engaged in a low-risk venture. Maybe we can cut costs without damage, or at least we know what the damage will be. This notion can be misguided, in some cases quite literally fatally so.

In 2005, BP's Texas City refinery suffered an explosion which resulted in 15 people being killed and 180 injured. A major contributing factor, according to the US Government's Chemical Safety Board, was a lack of preventive maintenance in the years leading up to the accident, in turn the result of a corporate directive to reduce costs by 25%. Think instead what would have happened had they been asked to increase capacity by 25%. This would have been a major capital project with a heavyweight project team, corporate oversight, risk management plan – the whole works. They would have done it very well. Instead, because it was cost reduction, there was none of this and the results were catastrophic.

The Texas City case illustrates, in the most graphic way possible, that there is always a simple way to cut costs – increase risk. It is very unlikely that anything you do to reduce costs in your business will result in 15 deaths and 180 injuries. The results will less dramatic, along the lines of:

- A gradual deterioration in the level of customer service as fewer people struggle to do more and more

- Falling quality resulting from ageing machinery and less time to check work

- Minor problems developing into major crises because everyone is so busy that nobody has time to spot them and nip them in the bud

- Slow attrition of key staff as they tire of having to do more and more with less and less.

All this happens gradually, until a dramatic event such as the defection of a major customer or a well-publicised product failure.

This is not an argument against cost reduction in all cases, but an argument for careful, planned cost reduction. Whatever you plan, assume that somehow, somewhere you are increasing risk. Be honest with yourself about what that risk is, and make sure that you have a plan to manage it as well as possible.

Beware the Snowball Effect

We tend to assume, also, that as we reduce costs the effects will be in proportion to the costs removed. If we trim costs by 5%, quality, service or sales will fall by at most 5%. This is comforting, as it means we can proceed gradually. Cut some, then if nothing too awful happens, cut some more. It's comforting, but wrong. We need to account for the snowball effect.

Here is an example. Imagine we have a customer service department which can handle 100 calls a day, and on an average day we receive 90 calls. Most days we can deal with everything that comes in, and on the days when we can't we can clear the backlog the next day. Now suppose that we reduce capacity in customer service to 90 per day. Sooner or later, we will have a day when we have 100 enquiries. We can't deal with all of these, so 10 need to wait for the next day. But the next day, of course, we have 90 new enquiries which, added to the 10 brought forward from the previous day, is more than we can handle.

We are not clearing the backlog, but it gets worse than that. Not only do we have more calls than we can deal with, but our capacity to deal with them is reducing. Customers are getting angry, and harder to deal with. Issues are being escalated, which absorbs more time. We start spending more time in meetings, discussing how to solve the problem. Senior management become aware of the issue, so we have to spend a lot of time compiling reports and briefings for them.

Pretty soon we have, on average 90 calls a day, a capacity to deal with only 70 and an ever-growing backlog. In short, we removed our safety margin so that a small fluctuation created a major crisis. In this example the small fluctuation was a day with 10 calls more than average, but it could have been an unusually large number of people off sick for a couple of days, or a small change to the product resulting in extra calls.

The point is, think of these situations as being like an elastic band. You can stretch it a little, and everything is fine. Then you can stretch it a bit more, and everything is still fine. Then a little more. But then – completely unexpectedly – it breaks. And it cannot be repaired.

The ROI Rule

To guide you through this hazardous area, remember the Return on Investment rule. This was given to me by a venture capitalist, on the board of a company where I was FD. It's one of the wisest pieces of advice I've heard.

"Any money you spend is an investment decision. It doesn't matter whether it's in the budget, or whether you spent it last year, or whether Fred has resigned and you need to recruit a replacement at the same level. The only reason for spending money is because it produces a return on investment, that's to say you get back more than you spend."

Applying the rule can help you in three ways:

1. it will help you cut further in areas that don't contribute

2. it will show you areas where you can in fact invest to improve performance

3. it will introduce some objectivity into what is often a very emotional and political process.

Using the ROI rule is a hugely superior method to salami-slicing 3% off everything, or imposing arbitrary targets without knowing what's really possible or what the impacts could be.

Case Study – How Not to Cut Costs

Mark was a partner in a firm of accountants. He developed a neat little piece of software for tax planning calculations. He initially just used it himself, but realised he could sell it to other firms. He paid £1,000 for an advert on the back page of Accountancy magazine, and sold £6,000 worth of software. Reasonably enough, he wanted to repeat the exercise. He went to his partners and asked for another £1,000 to run the ad again. Their response? "Sorry, can't do that. We've spent the marketing budget for the year."

This is not the way to reduce costs.

Examples of How to Use the ROI Rule

I have played this game with many Chief Executive groups, with fascinating results. I ask someone to think of a cost, any cost, that they have been trying to reduce, and instead think of reasons for increasing it.

Marketing Costs

A manufacturer of surgical equipment had a stand every year at the major trade fair. The previous year they had become bored with waiting on the stand for prospects to walk up to them, and one person had started wandering the halls approaching likely-looking people asking if they were interested in the company's products and whether they would like more information. They had managed to find about fifty likely prospects, and generated several worthwhile new leads. They were planning to send an extra person in the coming year, so as to have two people roaming the halls.

"Is two enough? I asked. "You managed to find 50 prospects last year. How many do you think there were at the show?" "Probably 10 times that," was the reply.

Well in that case, wouldn't you want to send 10 people? Think about it – here you have a concentrated assembly of prospects. The cost of sending an extra person is two days salary and accommodation – tiny compared to the value of even one new customer. Why wouldn't you send everyone available? It will surely be more profitable than anything else they could be doing in those two days.

Finance Department of a Law Firm

Most companies tend to think of their finance departments as necessary, if expensive, overhead. Even most finance directors think of their departments that way. What would happen if, instead, we looked at the finance department as an investment opportunity? I had the chance to try this out with the FD of a law firm.

"Suppose, I said, "you wanted to come up with an argument for doubling the cost of your department. What would you do?"

The first thing, he decided, would be to add one person to credit control. The economy was slowing, and like everyone else they were having to work harder to get paid. An extra person here would cost about £25,000. Given the size of the firm's overdraft they would probably save that much in interest, and having more cash in the bank would make it easier to do other things. Not a difficult decision.

The next recruitment would be an analyst. The firm, like any professional firm, had huge amounts of data on the time it was spending on each matter and each client, and the amount they were being paid. Unfortunately, nobody had time to look at or make sense of this data. One analyst, cost £35,000, would be able to do this. As a first step, they would be able to identify the fee-earners and clients who were not billing or being billed as they should. Resolving these issues would be worth, he estimated, about £125,000 a year. This was an excellent return on £35,000 but it was just the start. Really understanding where the firm made its money, the types of work and the types of client which made the most money, would enable it to develop the business in the most profitable way. Within a year or two, this would be worth £350,000 a year. We stopped at this point. The point had been made.

Fast Action Plan for Cost Reduction

Apply the ROI rule to everything. This will give you a good idea of where to start. You may have two different ideas for cutting costs, which both save you the same amount. The ROI rule may indicate that one will cost you more in terms of future revenues than the other, thus giving you clear guidance as to which to do first.

The other thing to do with the ROI rule, while you are using it, is to look for ways to spend more money. This will seem completely counter-intuitive when you are in a cost-cutting frame or mind, but it may be the better path.

If you need to cut spending, think of all the things you could do, and divide them into three categories:

1. Things which will almost certainly cause damage in the future, like reducing marketing or product development

2. Things which might cause damage in the future, but with a little luck might not. This would include things like a salaries freeze – you might lose some good people, but on the other hand, if you don't stretch it too far and keep a close eye on what's happening in the job market, you might not. For each of these actions, have a plan for managing the risk involved

3. Things which represent sustainable improvements or cost reductions. For instance, you might find a group of customers who are being served by field sales reps, but who don't place enough business to pay for the cost of those visits. If you can find a way of serving them by phone or over the web, that is a sustainable cost reduction.

Putting the different actions in the right category is not difficult, so long as you are honest with yourself. Now you can start to make decisions. Start with the Type Threes, moving on Type Twos if necessary, with the risk management plan. Only do Type Ones if you really have to.

Raising Efficiency

Not cutting costs. By this point most of the cost cutting work is done, but done in an intelligent way. By looking at product and customer profitability you have removed costs which go into unprofitable activity. By looking for spare capacity you have removed most surplus cost.

The most useful thing to do now is to apply the ROI rule:

Any money you spend is an investment. You don't spend it because it's in the budget, you don't spend it because you spent it last year, or because someone has resigned and you need to replace them with someone else at the same level. You spend it because it produces a return.

Start by looking at all the things you spend money on which are supposed to produce a benefit in the future, but for which that benefit is not always clearly identified. This means things like:

- Marketing – the acquisition of new customers

- Training

- Product development.

As you go through the areas, ask these questions:

- Can I actually prove, with reasonable certainty, that these areas of expenditure produce a positive return on investment?

- If I can, why are we not spending more in those areas?

- If I break down the total into its component parts (for example, total marketing into marketing in different media, or different target audiences), do I see differences in the returns from different parts?

- If so, what would happen if we reallocated resources from lower-productivity to higher-productivity uses?

The reality of most businesses is that these sorts of judgments are going to be quite subjective. It can be quite hard to assess the productivity of marketing, for example. Lots of stuff goes out, and new customers come in. It can be difficult to make the connection, but one thing is to estimate likely lifetime value of new customers and identify the best. Then at least ask the question of whether your current activities look most likely to produce those types of customers.

This is the opposite of salami-slicing. Applying the ROI rule will produce superior results for three reasons:

- It will enable you to cut more deeply in areas which aren't productive

- It will give you confidence to spend more in areas which will produce a return

- You will learn a lot of about what makes your business tick.

About the Author

Described as "an outstanding contrarian consultant" by the Institute of Business Consulting, consultant, speaker and author Alastair Dryburgh specialises in finding unusual solutions to common, intractable problems.

His firm, Akenhurst Consultants, works with clients who are frustrated with achieving average results from doing the usual things, or who see novel approaches as a way of achieving a competitive advantage.

For more details and a regular fix of
new, different ideas including a free
monthly teleconference, visit
www.alastairdryburgh.com [1]

2229912R00094

Printed in Great Britain
by Amazon.co.uk, Ltd.,
Marston Gate.